Government
and Society

Government
and Society

*Inside
Ancient
China*

ALASTAIR MORRISON

Sharpe Focus
an imprint of M.E. Sharpe, Inc.

First edition for the United States, its territories and dependencies,
Canada, Mexico, and Australia, published in 2009

Sharpe Focus
An imprint of M.E. Sharpe, Inc.
80 Business Park Drive
Armonk, NY 10504

www.sharpe-focus.com

Library of Congress Cataloging-in-Publication Data

Morrison, Alastair.
  Government and society / Alastair Morrison.
    p. cm. -- (Inside ancient China)
  Includes bibliographical references and index.
  ISBN 978-0-7656-8166-9 (hardcover : alk. paper)
 1. China--Politics and government--To 221 B.C.--Juvenile literature. 2.
China--Politics and government--221 B.C.-960 A.D.--Juvenile literature. 3.
China--Politics and government--960-1279--Juvenile literature. 4.
China--Social conditions--To 221 B.C.--Juvenile literature. 5.
China--Social conditions--221 B.C.-960 A.D.--Juvenile literature. 6.
China--Social conditions--960-1644--Juvenile literature. I. Title.

  JQ1510.M67 2009
  306.20951'0902--dc22

                            2008031166

Editorial and design by Amber Books Ltd
Project Editor: James Bennett
Consultant Editor: Susan Whitfield
Copy Editor: Constance Novis
Picture Research: Terry Forshaw, Natascha Spargo
Design: Joe Conneally

Cover Design: Jesse M. Sanchez, M.E. Sharpe, Inc.

Printed in Malaysia

9 8 7 6 5 4 3 2 1

PICTURE CREDITS
All photographs and illustrations courtesy of Shanghai Scientific and
Technological Literature Publishing House except for the following:

AKG Images: 43
Alamy: 48 (Classic Stock)
Art Archive: 14 (Bibliothèque Nationale, Paris), 32/33 (National Palace
Museum, Taiwan), 42 (top, Freer Gallery of Art), 46/47 (National Palace
Museum, Taiwan), 72/73 (National Palace Museum, Taiwan), 74 (Musée
Cernuschi Paris / Dagli Orti), 75 (Genius of China Exhibition)
Bridgeman Art Library: 38 (Bibliotheque Nationale, Paris/Archives
Charmet), 40 (Musée Guimet, Paris/Archives Charmet), 49 (British
Museum)

Corbis: 8 (Burstein Collection), 16/17 (John T. Young), 22 (Burstein
Collection), 24 (Bohemian Nomad Picturemakers), 35 (Carl & Ann
Purcell), 50 (Pierre Colombel), 56/57 (Royal Ontario Museum), 64
(Burstein Collection), 67 (Burstein Collection)
Dorling Kindersley: 58/59
Getty Images: 44 (China Span RM), 61 (China Span RM)
Photolibrary: 41, 45
Werner Forman Archive: 70 (National Palace Museum, Taipei)

All artworks courtesy of Laszlo Veres, Beehive Illustration
© Amber Books
All maps courtesy of Mark Franklin © Amber Books

ABOUT THE AUTHOR
Alastair Morrison works at the British Library on the International
Dunhuang Project (IDP) managing the project's overseas offices in
China and Russia. He is completing a Ph.D. on Chinese literature
at the School of Oriental and African Studies (SOAS), University of
London. He has written educational resources on China and the
Silk Road for IDP, and is engaged in developing IDP's educational
resources. He has taught Chinese to London schoolchildren and
Masters-level translation courses at SOAS. He worked as a
consultant on Chinese culture and history for the thriller novel
Tokyo by Mo Hayder, and has spent three years working and
studying in China.

Contents

Introduction

China is the world's oldest continuous civilization, originating in the plains and valleys of the Yellow and Yangtze rivers more than six thousand years ago. In the third century B.C.E., the separate kingdoms of China were united to form an empire. Over the centuries China was ruled by a series of ruling houses, or families, known as dynasties. The empire was governed by an emperor, who was advised by highly educated scholars and who commanded a strong army. No dynasty lasted for more than a few hundred years and several were founded by invaders, such as the Mongol Yuan Dynasty and the Manchu Qing Dynasty. Successive dynasties expanded Chinese territory, until the empire extended into the northern steppes, the western deserts, and the southern tropics, reaching the extent of the China we know today.

China was not always united. Often the fall of dynasties resulted in long periods where different groups competed for power. Dynasties sometimes overlapped, each controlling a part of China. Throughout all these periods, the rulers retained classical Chinese as the official language, and many dynasties saw great cultural and technological developments. Through ancient trade routes and political missions, Chinese culture reached the rest of Asia, Europe, and Africa. Chinese technologies—including the compass, paper, gunpowder, and printing—had a profound effect on civilization throughout Eurasia. China was, in turn, greatly influenced by its neighbors, resulting in a diverse and complex civilization.

Government and Society

A vast land made up of different peoples and cultures, China required a sophisticated system of government to maintain order. The ancient Chinese developed an efficient system which employed professional civil servants, recruited by examinations, supported by a strong army. Local magistrates ruled over far-flung corners of the empire by working with existing local leaders. Newly conquered lands were controlled by military governors. Foreign rulers of China all adopted the same system and employed many Chinese officials. A legal code was applied throughout the Chinese empire and, for much of its history, the death penalty was rare. Special government officials called censors could criticize the emperor if they disagreed with his decisions, and individual officials could also submit criticisms, although they risked losing their jobs or being exiled if they were too harsh. Each emperor and dynasty only retained its right to rule, called the "Mandate of Heaven," if it was seen to rule morally and correctly. Dynasties fell when the public felt they had lost the Mandate of Heaven by acting unreasonably, cruelly, or immorally. The dynastic system and the recruitment exams for civil servants lasted until the early twentieth century.

The Main Dynasties of China

Shang   c. 1600–c. 1050 B.C.E.
Zhou   c. 1050–221 B.C.E.

The Zhou Dynasty can be divided into:
        Western Zhou   1050–771 B.C.E.
        Eastern Zhou   770–221 B.C.E.

The Eastern Zhou Dynasty can also be divided into the
following periods:
        Spring and Autumn Period   770–476 B.C.E.
        Warring States Period   475–221 B.C.E.

Qin   221–206 B.C.E.
Han   206 B.C.E.–220 C.E.

From 221 C.E. to 589 C.E., different regions of China were
ruled by several different dynasties and emperors in a
period of disunity.

Sui   589–618 C.E.
Tang   618–907 C.E.

There was another period of disunity between the Tang
and Song dynasties.

Song   960–1279 C.E.
Yuan   1279–1368 C.E.
Ming   1368–1644 C.E.
Qing   1644–1911 C.E.

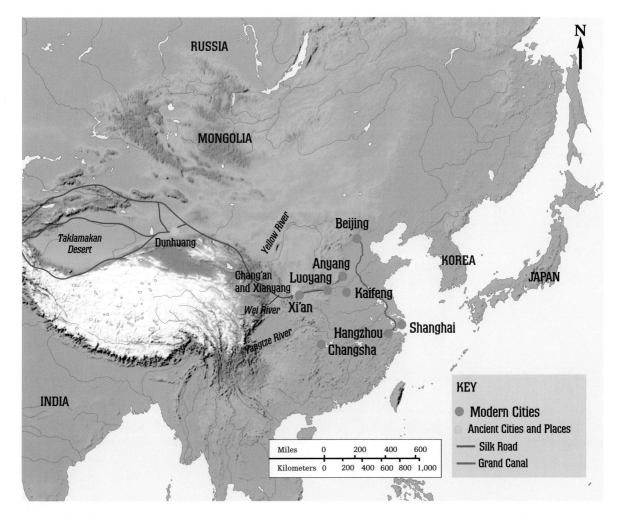

This map shows the major present-day and ancient cities and regions mentioned throughout this book, along with the eastern part of the Silk Road and the Grand Canal linking Beijing with Hangzhou.

武帝字文邕在
八年五帝共廿五年
佛法

Chapter One

Early China

China's first recorded dynasty was the Shang (c. 1600–1050 B.C.E.), which dominated the Yellow River valley in the second millennium B.C.E. Historical writings of later dynasties and modern archaeological discoveries have provided a wealth of information about this society. However, even though it was primarily an agricultural civilization, little is known about the peasants of this period. Most of our knowledge of the Shang involves rulers and aristocrats.

The Xia: China's Earliest Dynasty?

Sima Qian (*Suh-mar-chee'en*), China's first great historian, records the Xia (*Shee'ah*) Dynasty (1900–1350 B.C.E.) as China's first dynasty. There has been much debate over this claim however, and for a while scholars considered the Xia to be more mythical than real. No written records of the Xia Dynasty have been found, which has led many historians to consider the Shang Dynasty as China's first historical dynasty. However, excavations in 1959 at Erlitou (*Err-lee-toe*) in Henan province revealed palaces and tombs that archaeologists are beginning to identify with the Xia Dynasty. Historians see the first three dynasties of ancient China, the Xia, Shang, and Zhou (*Joe*) as initially existing together at the same time, then gradually replacing each other. There were many other states in China at this time, but these were the most powerful. Therefore it now looks very likely that the Xia Dynasty did indeed exist, but there are still no written records from that period to prove it, only tentative evidence from archaeology such as palaces and bronzes.

This seventh-century image shows Emperor Wu, who lived from 543–578 C.E., with his attendants. Wu was the leader of one of the short-lived states that controlled parts of China during the period of disunity after the end of the Han Dynasty.

Shang Dynasty bronze vessels were often decorated with images of animals and were used for cooking or for rituals. This is a three-footed *ding* vessel, or cauldron, with crouching tigers on its "ears."

The Shang rulers only had limited control over their territory. They occupied a series of capitals, but the most important was at Anyang in present-day Henan province. Power came from the king's armies and was concentrated in the capital and the few places that the king visited regularly. Shang inscriptions portray the Zhou people, who lived 420 miles (675 kilometers) from Anyang, as subjects of the Shang, but it is clear from other sources that the

Predicting the Future

The Shang people worshipped their ancestors. They held rituals to communicate with the "first ancestor," *di*, as well as other ancestors, and to ask questions about the future. They also practiced divination: attempting to foretell or foresee the future by interpreting omens. To do this they would scratch questions onto shoulder bones of oxen or the plastrons (breastbones) of tortoises. The bones were given to a diviner, who held a high position as advisor to the king. During a divination session the diviner would be asked various questions. Small pits or holes were then chiseled into the bone. The diviner applied a heat source into the pit until the bone cracked. The shapes of the cracks were interpreted as an answer to the question. The king himself would sometimes perform oracle bone divinations, often to ask about the right time to go to war.

Zhou did not consider themselves to be subjects of the Shang and had few dealings with them. The Zhou had a separate kingdom of their own, and there were other independent kingdoms in the south and north.

The Shang Dynasty had a clearly defined class structure. At the top were the king and royal family. Under the aristocracy were craftsmen, many of whom were bronze workers. They lived more comfortably than the peasants, in houses made of compacted dirt, with two rooms and sometimes with a window. At the bottom of the social ladder were peasants, who farmed but also hunted and raised animals for food.

Kings and nobles of the Shang Dynasty lived in great style, so it was natural that when they died they wanted to be buried with the same beautiful objects for use in the afterlife. Many of these objects were ceremonial vessels made of bronze, which were sophisticated in technology and design. One typical form was the *jue* (*Joo'eh*), a ritual vessel on three legs, used for warming wine. The surfaces of the vessels were covered with stylized decorations and inscriptions detailing the reason they had been cast and their intended use.

The Zhou and the Warring States

Historical records describe how the Shang were defeated by the Zhou people from the Wei River valley in about 1050 B.C.E. Although Shang forces were greater in number than the invading Zhou, the Zhou historians recorded

Dragon Bones

Bones used by Shang diviners were discovered by accident in the early twentieth century when a Chinese scholar rescued them from pharmacies in Beijing where they were being sold as "dragon bones" to cure malaria. Archaeologists then found many thousands of oracle bones in the ground around the ancient capital of Anyang on the Yellow River. Tombs of kings and nobles containing many exquisite bronze artifacts were also excavated.

Questions about the future were carved on ox bones like this. These bones contain the earliest known form of Chinese writing, which has come to be known as Oracle Bone script.

that Shang soldiers joined the Zhou armies because of the cruelty of their ruler. However, it was common for historians of a successful dynasty to write about how cruel the ruler of the previous dynasty had been.

The new dynasty, later known as the Western Zhou, then ruled from 1050–771 B.C.E. It had its capital in a large walled city at Zhengzhou (*Jung-joe*) on the Yellow River. The ruling class of the Zhou was like a large extended family, and at first the nobles were loyal to the king. Peoples living under the influence of Zhou culture began to feel a common identity that could be considered "Chinese." The Western Zhou Dynasty came to an end in 771 B.C.E. when non-Chinese northern peoples, in alliance with rebellious Chinese states, invaded its territory. Natural disasters, such as earthquakes and famines, also undermined the Zhou. As a result the capital was moved east along the river valley to Luoyang (*Lwoh-yang*), where their rule continued during a period called the Eastern Zhou Dynasty.

The early period of the Eastern Zhou Dynasty from 770–476 B.C.E. is now known as the Spring and Autumn Period, after a history book of the period called the *Annals of Spring and Autumn*. During this early period, northern China was divided into approximately fifteen states. The Eastern Zhou controlled the area around its new capital, Luoyang, though its influence was exercised mainly through religious ceremonies rather than actual political power. Around this time, the use of bronze and iron increased and was used for coins, utensils, weapons, and agricultural tools. Communications on land and water also improved. Relations between the different states were mostly friendly during this period, although they were unable to present a united front to threats from invaders from the north and west.

Zhou authority eventually weakened, and power struggles developed in some states leading to the overthrow of some noble families. This marked the beginning of the Warring States Period, which lasted from 475 B.C.E. until unification of China by the Qin (*Chin*) in 221 B.C.E. By the beginning of the 200s B.C.E., there were three major states fighting for power, the Qin, Chu (*Choo*), and Qi. Rivalries between these states intensified, leading to a change in warfare from small campaigns led by nobles to large-scale wars. Iron weapons and the crossbow began to be used, and cavalry were introduced so that the Chinese armies could fight the horse-riding nomads who threatened their northern and western borders.

Although war was more frequent in this period, trade within China continued to grow. This can be seen from the spread of bronze coinage. Coins, including spade coins, coins in the form of a knife, and a round coin pierced by a hole, were minted in all the major states. By 231 B.C.E. the Qin had defeated their last rivals for control of the region, and by 221 B.C.E. had established a centralized empire in China for the first time.

Qin Shi Huangdi, the First Emperor

The man who became the first emperor of China was given the name Zheng (*Jung*), which means upright or correct. He was born in 259 B.C.E., the son of the king of Qin (*Chin*) and a concubine. Concubines were additional wives who had lower status than a man's main wife. Zheng became king of Qin in 246 B.C.E. at the age of thirteen when his father died. During his reign, the armies of Qin defeated all the other neighboring kingdoms, and from 221 B.C.E., the king of Qin ruled over all of China. He then called himself Qin Shi Huangdi (*Chin Shuh-Hwang-di*), or the First Emperor Qin. Qin was the state where he was born. Shi means "first," and "Huangdi" means emperor, where *huang* means noble or honored and *di* refers to the original ancestor worshipped during the Shang Dynasty (c. 1600–1050 B.C.E.), thus giving the emperor's new title a godlike, majestic quality.

First Emperor Qin united China for the first time, and standardized much of daily life in the new empire. He is often believed to have begun building the Great Wall of China, but in fact he extended existing walls that had been put in place by different states across northern China. Because he was now ruling over such a large territory, he introduced new laws and a system of bureaucracy that, in a modified form, would last for 2,000 years. He traveled extensively over his empire and left writings on stone at places where he had visited or made sacrifices.

The First Emperor was superstitious and toward the end of his life ordered his ministers to search for a medicine that would allow him to live forever. Some historians think he took mixtures of minerals that included gold, mercury, sulfur, and lead. Like all rulers and aristocrats of his time, First Emperor Qin was concerned that his tomb be both grand and suitable for the afterlife. Once he had settled into ruling his new empire, he ordered the construction of his tomb. At one time, 700,000 convicts and forced laborers were working either on his new palace or his tomb. The tomb is a four-sided pyramid originally 394 feet (120 meters) high, although now it is only 210 feet (64 meters) high because it has been eroded over the centuries. He finally died in 210 B.C.E. during one of his journeys around the empire.

No one knows for sure what the First Emperor looked like. Artists have depicted him over the centuries, testifying to his importance in Chinese history.

Qin Law Code

The Qin law code was applied throughout the empire. The basic principles were to obey the law, and to report other people breaking the law. Many Qin laws were very severe to enforce obedience. People who did not report criminals could also be punished for the crime. When archaeologists discovered the tomb of Lady Dai at Changsha in Hunan province, they found manuscripts of the Qin legal code. These showed examples of moderate laws being fairly applied in different situations, showing that the law was not always harsh and cruel. The First Emperor issued official communications called edicts to impose his new laws on standardization across the empire. All the edicts were written in a new script developed by Li Si, the First Emperor's advisor. This script was based on the form of writing originally used in the state of Qin, and was made obligatory across the empire. Edicts written in the new script were carved onto rocks at sacred mountains, such as Mount Tai in present-day Shandong province.

This bronze mold is inscribed with the edicts of the First and Second Emperors.

The Qin Dynasty (221–206 B.C.E.): A United Empire

The Qin state was located along the Wei River, a tributary of the Yellow River. At its height it had a population of around 40 million people. The name "*Qin*" (pronounced *Chin*) gave China its modern name in English. The ruler of Qin called himself the First Emperor and made many changes to Chinese society during his reign.

The First Emperor Qin (259–210 B.C.E.) ordered his relatives and other nobles to leave their country manors and come to live in the capital Xianyang (*Shee'en-yang*), near present-day Xi'an (*Shee'ann*), where he could control them more easily. According to the historical records, 120,000 families were ordered to move. The empire was then divided into 36 units, each of which was ruled by three officials, supervised directly by the emperor.

Keeping an Empire Together

Many aspects of life in the Qin Dynasty (221–206 B.C.E.) were standardized to ensure clear communication across such a large empire. Standard measures and weights were introduced. The wheels of carts and chariots had to be the same width, which made

The First Emperor Qin tried to control his new empire as closely as possible, often by violent means. This painting shows his soldiers burning books and burying scholars who he had ordered to be killed.

1600 B.C.E.		1000 B.C.E.		
Shang Dynasty 1600–1050 B.C.E.		Western Zhou Dynasty 1050–771 B.C.E.	Spring and Autumn Period	

building roads easier and travel quicker, because the ruts made by the wheels were the same distance apart. More than 4,000 miles (6,500 kilometers) of new roads were built, of which five were main imperial roads intended for fast communication.

Chinese writing had evolved naturally over hundreds of years. Individual states and peoples with different languages had different ways of writing the same character or word. Introducing one system of writing to transcribe the official language began under the Qin Dynasty (221–206 B.C.E.), although people continued to use different forms even during later dynasties. Money was also standardized, and gold and copper coins were put into circulation.

First Emperor Qin tried to keep strict control on knowledge, and suppressed opinions that differed from his own. It is said that he ordered the burning of all books apart from practical texts on law, medicine, pharmacy, divination, and agriculture. In fact, scholars who

The First Emperor Qin ordered his relatives to move to the capital. These tombs near Xi'an in central China have not been excavated and possibly contain relatives of the First Emperor.

Warring States Period		500 C.E.	
	Han Dynasty 206 B.C.E.–220 C.E.	Period of Disunity	
Qin Dynasty 221–206 B.C.E.			

worked for the emperor were allowed to keep copies of the banned books, so many were later restored during the Han Dynasty (206 B.C.E.–220 C.E.).

The death of First Emperor Qin in 210 B.C.E. presented the problem of finding someone to succeed him. Officials were worried about unrest breaking out when the news spread that the emperor had died, so they transported his body back to the capital surrounded by containers of fish to disguise the smell of his rotting corpse. Finally, the emperor's son Er Shi took over as Second Emperor Qin at the age of twenty-one. The people were unhappy at the heavy taxation that was required to build him a new imperial palace, so a peasant named Chen Sheng started a revolt. He was soon killed but the rebellion continued, and eventually amid much bloodshed the Qin Dynasty was wiped out and its palace at Xianyang burned to the ground.

The Han Dynasty (206 B.C.E.–220 C.E.): Chinese Culture Flourishes

After the end of the Qin Dynasty (221–206 B.C.E.), two generals, Xiangyu (*Shee'ang-yoo*) and Liu Bang, contended for power over China. A civil war between the two generals began, with Liu Bang defeating Xiangyu in 202 B.C.E. at Gaixia (*Guy-shee'ah*) in present-day Anhui (*Ann-hweh*)

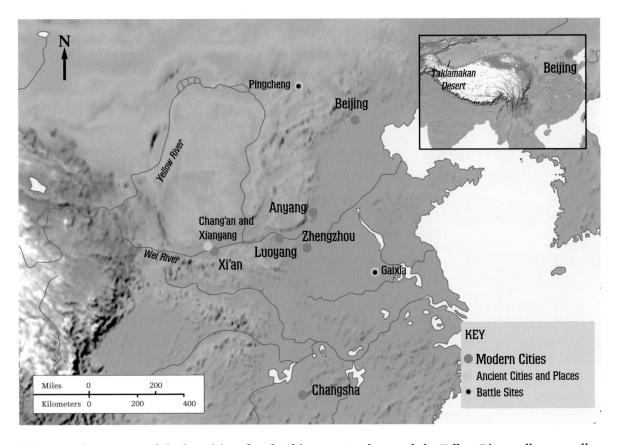

This map shows some of the key cities of early China, centered around the Yellow River valley, as well as the location of the Taklamakan desert in western China.

Relations with the Steppe

In 209 B.C.E. the Xiongnu (*Shee'ong-noo*), a people who lived on the steppe, or flat grassland, to the northwest of China, united under their leader Maodun and invaded Chinese territory. Emperor Gaozu (*Gao-tzuh*) tried to reclaim the land they had taken, but was defeated and nearly captured at the Battle of Pingcheng in 200 B.C.E. He then changed his strategy from war to diplomacy. Treaties were signed between the Han and Xiongnu, and for each treaty a marriage alliance was arranged between a Han princess and a Xiongnu leader. This reduced the risk of attack and led to trade across borders.

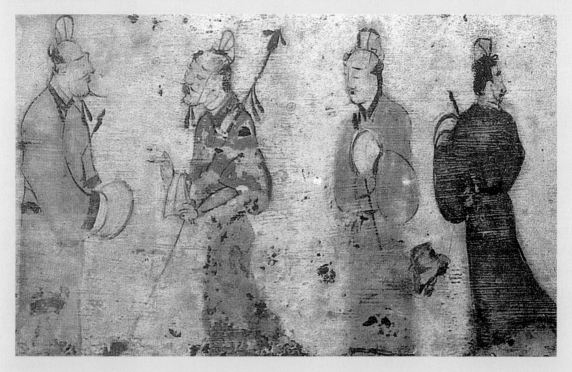

Showing respect in formal situations was important in ancient China, as it still is today. This Han Dynasty painting shows guests paying homage to a high-ranking official.

province. Liu Bang became emperor, becoming known as Emperor Gaozu (*Gao-tzuh*) after his death. He made his walled capital at Chang'an, southwest of Xianyang. This was the beginning of the Han Dynasty.

As the first emperor of the Han Dynasty, Liu Bang (c. 247–195 B.C.E.) introduced new rules that made the imperial system more stable and less likely to be defeated by rebellions or invasions. He extended the Qin Dynasty's bureaucracy and kept its legal institutions. This meant that peasants still had to pay household tax and land tax, as well as having to labor on public works and serve in the army. These obligations were less of a burden during the Han than Qin, however. Construction of the Han capital Chang'an, which began under Gaozu, was continued by his successors.

At this time, because of the growing population and lack of available land, people began to farm very intensively. As the Chinese empire expanded into neighboring territories to the south and west, the state relocated groups of farmers to the new lands. In the west they were sent to irrigate the desert and grow crops. These would be used to feed the armies that were stationed there and who passed through on campaigns further west.

After Emperor Gaozu died in 195 B.C.E., he was succeeded by a series of child emperors. They were too young to reign effectively, so their mother, Empress Lü (*Loo*) (?–180 B.C.E.), ruled in their place and provided stability to the Han Dynasty.

Later, under Emperor Wu Di (*Woo-di*) who reigned from 141–87 B.C.E., the Han generals finally managed to defeat the Xiongnu (*Shee'ong-noo*) and open a route westwards from the capital near Xi'an to the kingdoms around the Taklamakan Desert. Wu Di sent a military governor to control the region and established military garrisons and fortifications, often using older walls. Many influential books in Chinese history were written during Wu Di's reign, and the teachings of Confucius now provided the moral and political beliefs of the state.

The Han Dynasty was suspended briefly when a prince named Wang Mang (45 B.C.E.–23 C.E.) seized the throne in 9 C.E. He tried to restrict the power of the landowners by redistributing land to the poor and freeing slaves. Two years later a huge flood of the Yellow River destroyed many peasants' homes and crops. The starving peasants rebelled against the government. Powerful landowners crushed the rebellion, defeated the government troops, and killed Wang Mang. They re-established the Han Dynasty, with its capital further east, in Luoyang. This new line of emperors was known as the Eastern Han Dynasty, which lasted from 25–220 C.E.

Period of Disunity

A century before it finally ended, the Han Dynasty was in turmoil. There were frequent rebellions and violent deaths at court. Also, the gap was growing between rich and poor. The Han collapsed

Emperors had many concubines in ancient China. This Ming Dynasty (1368–1644 C.E.) painting shows a Han Dynasty palace artist painting portraits of the emperor's concubines.

in 220 C.E., and for 300 years no single dynasty had control over all of China. At first there were three kingdoms, the Wei, Shu, and Wu, but China split further in 280 C.E. In 311 C.E. the Xiongnu plundered and ravaged Luoyang and until 589 C.E. China was divided between dynasties of the south, which tried to revive the tradition of the Han, and dynasties of the north that were ruled by other, non-Chinese peoples. This period is therefore called the Southern and Northern Dynasties (420–589 C.E.) It was an age of civil war and disunity, but one which also saw advances in medicine, military technology, and the arts.

Chapter Two

China's Golden Age

The Sui Dynasty (589–618 C.E.) united China again for the first time after 250 years of disunity. The founder of the Sui was a northern general called Yang Jian (*Yang-jee'en*) (541–604 C.E.), who defeated the last of the southern dynasties in 589 C.E. He wanted to recreate the traditions of the Han Dynasty (206 B.C.E.–220 C.E.). In order to justify taking power, he forged a document he claimed the last emperor had written on his deathbed asking Yang Jian to take charge of the military and assist the child emperor. When he took power, Jian took the name Emperor Wen. He supported the two influential schools of thought at the time, Confucianism and Buddhism. He rewarded those who showed Confucian moral virtues, and he gave generously to the Buddhist clergy and temples, promoting Buddhism as a faith of the ordinary people.

Three Streams of Thought

Chinese culture was influenced by three main schools of thought, Confucianism, Daoism, and Buddhism. Often people would lean towards one school at different times in their lives. Confucianism believed man's nature was naturally good, and stressed harmony in families and, by extension, across society. Daoism regarded harmony with nature as the ultimate good and sought freedom from convention. Buddhism was a religion from India and taught that people would be reincarnated (born again) in future lives and that by doing good deeds in this life they could hope for a better next life.

China enjoyed great prosperity after being reunited by the Sui Dynasty. This painting shows Emperor Wen of the Sui Dynasty with two attendants.

Emperor Wen of the Sui Dynasty (589–618 C.E.) ordered a fleet of *Wuya* (five-toothed) battleships to be built to defeat the Chen Dynasty (557–589 C.E.) on the Yangtze River. A *Wuya* battleship could hold 800 soldiers.

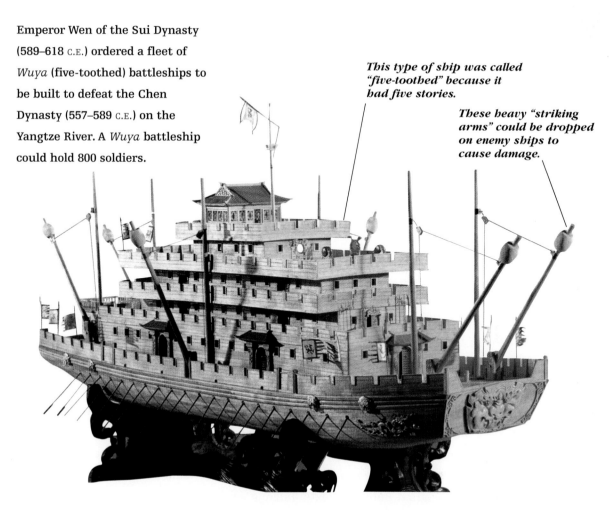

This type of ship was called "five-toothed" because it had five stories.

These heavy "striking arms" could be dropped on enemy ships to cause damage.

Emperor Wen built a new city on the old site of Chang'an, which had previously been a Chinese capital. He recruited new officials from all over the empire, both Chinese and non-Chinese. During his reign the examination system for recruiting officials began, and in 587 C.E. he ordered every region to send three men each year to the capital to be selected for official posts. Wen also reformed the law and improved the tax system. Common people had to pay land tax, a payment in silk or linen, and each adult male had to labor on government projects for twenty days per year.

Once it was in full control of the north, the Sui began to confiscate weapons and reorganize its army, improving the security of China's border areas to the north and south. Wen improved communications across the empire, making it easier to rule. His most famous project was the building of the Grand Canal that linked Chang'an to the Yellow River, improving the supply of grain to the capital.

The Grand Canal is the longest ancient canal in the world. Although parts of it date from the fifth century B.C.E., it was largely built by Emperor Wen of the Sui Dynasty.

After 609 C.E., the second Sui emperor launched military campaigns beyond China's borders into the kingdoms in Vietnam in the south, those of the Turks to the north, and into the Korean kingdoms in the northeast. Rebellions broke out in China after the campaign in Korea failed. The emperor was killed and in 618 C.E. one of the rebel generals, Li Yuan, declared himself emperor of a new dynasty called the Tang, which lasted from 618–907 C.E.

The Tang Dynasty (618–907 C.E.)

The rulers of the Tang were of mixed Chinese and northern ancestry, and under their governance, China was open to outside influences. Buddhism and other foreign religions flourished, and great accomplishments were also made in poetry and the arts. Tang influence extended from the borders of Persia and Central Asia to Japan in the east. By 624 C.E. the Tang had gained full control of the empire. The new emperor, who was now known as Gaozu (566–635 C.E.), brought in new government systems, which laid the foundations for the later success of the dynasty. He introduced a coinage that became standard throughout the Tang Dynasty. He also began a revival of Confucianism and Daoism, but limited the influence of Buddhism.

In 626 C.E. one of Gaozu's sons, Li Shimin, murdered one of his brothers and arranged for one of his other brothers to be killed. He put pressure on his father to give up the throne and became Emperor Taizong. He appointed talented ministers to advise him, which was later seen as a model for the relationship between officials and the emperor. Taizong was initially distrustful of the power of the Buddhist priests in China. However, in 645 C.E. when the Chinese monk Xuanzang (*Shoo'ann-tzang*) returned from sixteen years of traveling to and living in India to gather original Buddhist texts, Taizong was so impressed that he promoted more favorable policies toward the Buddhist community. Taizong ruled until his death in 649 C.E., when his son became the third Tang emperor, Gaozong.

Seven years after Gaozong's death, his wife seized the throne, becoming Empress Wu Zetian (625–705 C.E.). Disaster struck in 695 C.E. when the Qidan (*Chee-dan*) people in the northeast rebelled and seized the area around present-day Beijing. This prompted the northern Turks and Tibetans to raid China. The empress was forced to bribe the Turks through an imperial marriage, which put an end to the Qidan rebellion. In 697 C.E. the empress began to favor two young brothers at court. They behaved so arrogantly toward officials and abused their power so much that charges of corruption were brought against them. The empress tried to intervene on their behalf, which led senior officials to murder the brothers and force the empress to give up the throne in 705.

Emperor Xuanzong (*Shoo'ann-tzong*) (685–762 C.E.) then took the throne. He found state finances in a shambles after years of corruption under Empress Wu. He therefore forbade women in the palace to wear precious jewelry in order to reduce palace expenditure. He

Cosmopolitan China

During Gaozong's reign (649–683 C.E.) the Chinese empire reached its furthest extent. By 659 C.E. it had military bases in the foothills of the Pamir mountains in the west (in present-day Tajikistan), and in the northeast the state of Koguryo (in present-day Korea) fell under Chinese control. The trade routes from China into the heart of Central Asia had grown since they were opened during the Han Dynasty (206 B.C.E.–220 C.E.), but in the Tang Dynasty (618–907 C.E.) goods and peoples began to move across great distances in all directions. Exotic animals, food, and such luxury items as jade were sold in the markets in Chang'an and other Chinese towns. Merchants from Central Asia formed their own communities and worshipped at their own temples in Chinese towns. Foreign storytellers and dancers would provide entertainment and bring news of desert oasis towns and stunning cave complexes of Buddhist art. Women enjoyed great freedoms compared to other periods of Chinese history. For example, aristocratic women played polo wearing Turkish caps and men's riding clothes. Artistic influences from Central Asian oasis kingdoms, Persia, and India could all be seen in household objects and crafts. This far-reaching power did not last long, however, because before the end of Gaozong's reign in 683 C.E., Chinese power started to decline in Central Asia and Korea.

During the Tang Dynasty many foreign peoples came to China. This wall painting at the Mogao Caves in Dunhuang, northwest China, shows foreign dignitaries distinguished by their styles of dress and skin color.

An Lushan Rebellion

During the reign of Emperor Xuanzong, great power and wealth had become concentrated in the hands of the *jiedushi* (*Jee'eh-doo'shuh*), the regional military commanders. This was originally intended to prevent foreign invasion, although this weakened the central authority of the emperor, giving rise to a series of events. In the 740s C.E. the Chinese lost a series of battles against the Tibetans for territory in present-day Pakistan. Around 750 C.E., the Tang had to give up territory in the southwest to the kingdom of Nanchao, in present-day Vietnam. In 751 C.E. Tang armies led by the Korean general Gao Xianzhi (*Gao-shee'ann-zhir*) were defeated at the western point of Tang control in Central Asia by the Arabs at the Talas River, in present-day Kazakhstan. Xuanzong neglected the affairs of state after becoming devoted to the concubine Yang Guifei (*Yang-gweh-fey*), who gave important government posts to her family. She made her cousin Yang Guozhong (*Yang-go-jong*) prime minister ahead of An Lushan, a half-Sogdian, half-Turkish general.

All this sparked a rebellion in 755 C.E., led by An Lushan. His armies took over Chang'an and Luoyang. An Lushan died in 757 C.E., but the rebellion continued for many years. Due to the crisis, soldiers protecting the trading routes through the desert oasis towns of the northwest had to be recalled to central China to help fight the rebellion. As a result the Tibetans took control of the area and their armies reached as far east as Chang'an. The Tibetans were pushed back with the help of the Turkish Uighurs, but they controlled the northwestern oasis towns for eighty years, sealing off trade from Central Asia to Tang China.

increased revenues by taking registers of people who had fled south to avoid hardships in the north, and making sure they were taxed. Tang rulers had taken several surveys of the population, called censuses, throughout the dynasty. In 742, the census revealed that the population in China was about fifty million.

Xuanzong's reign was one of great prosperity for most people. An expanded system of granaries, or grain warehouses, meant that officials could store grain and sell it cheaply when prices were high. More land was reclaimed for agriculture and improvements to the canal system made it easier to transport grain and other goods. Law and order were well maintained and trade was protected.

After the An Lushan rebellion, the Tang Dynasty recovered briefly in the ninth century. When famines occurred in northern China, however, rebels pillaged the richest towns and caused great devastation. The rebel leader, called Huang Chao, occupied Luoyang in 880 C.E. Later, one of Huang Chao's lieutenants, Zhu Wen, founded a new dynasty called the Later Liang Dynasty (907–923 C.E.) at the eastern city of Kaifeng. This date marks the end of the Tang Dynasty, which had lost all real power beginning in 885 C.E. Another period of civil war then followed.

The Five Dynasties and Ten Kingdoms Period (907–960 C.E.)

After the fall of the Tang, the military commanders and their armies divided China and formed their own separate dynasties. This period is known as the Five Dynasties and Ten Kingdoms Period. The Five Dynasties in the north quickly succeeded each other, none of them lasting long. They all used Kaifeng, on the Yellow River and east of Chang'an, as their capital city. The Ten Kingdoms in the south all existed together, and although it was not as turbulent as the north, they still suffered from periods of warfare.

During this time, China's civil service—tax and local government officials—continued routine administration in both northern and southern China despite the changing of dynasties. The kingdoms of the south were able to trade with foreign countries. Technical innovation and economic growth followed. The kingdom of Min in Fujian became rich by exporting silks and ceramics by sea. The kingdom of Chu around Changsha exported silk and cloth, and obtained a large income from selling tea to the north. The north, however, did not prosper because it was continually at war.

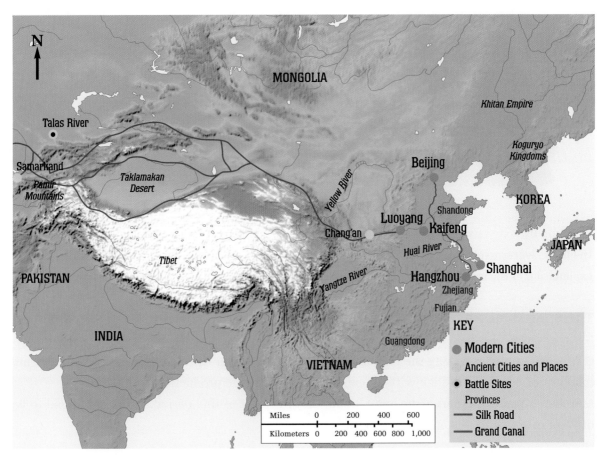

This map shows the key places in China and surrounding regions mentioned in this chapter. At its furthest extent, the Tang Dynasty's influence reached as far as Central Asia and Japan.

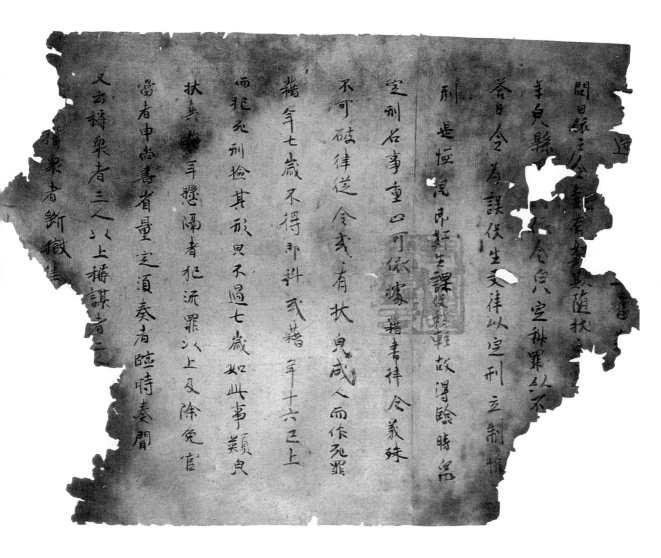

The Tang Dynasty saw the introduction of a complex new set of laws across China. In order to make the laws clearer to ordinary people, Emperor Gaozong ordered a team of scholars to write an explanation of the main points of the new laws. This manuscript contains these explanations.

The Song Dynasty (960–1279 C.E.)

Great changes occurred in political, social, economic, and intellectual life from the eleventh to thirteenth centuries, laying the foundations for China to enter the modern world. There was an increase of population along with an expansion of economic production and activity. Merchants traded both at home and abroad. But for most of this period, China continued to be divided into two halves, north and south.

General Zhao (*Jow*) (927–976 C.E.) founded the Song Dynasty in 960 C.E. at Kaifeng, having defeated most of the other independent kingdoms. Military expansion was limited to Chinese lands, and was stopped in the northeast by the powerful Khitan Empire, in the northwest by the Tibetans, and in the southwest by the Dali kingdom and an independent Vietnamese dynasty. In the reign of the third Song emperor, Zhengzong (*Jeng-tzong*), the Khitan Empire of the Liao (*Lee'ow*) forced the Song to sign a treaty obliging them to pay heavy tribute to the Liao. In the northwest, the large area had come under the sway of the Tanguts (*Tan-guts*), who ruled over a mixed population of Tibetan, Chinese, Turkish, and Mongol peoples. The threat they presented grew worse during the second half of the eleventh century.

In 1068 an official named Wang Anshi made reforms in the tax system, the economy, the military, and the administration. These reforms ended in a rebellion by rich landowners and merchants, however, and Wang Anshi lost power in 1085 C.E. after the death of his patron, Emperor Shenzong (1048–1085 C.E.). Power struggles continued until the invasion of the Jurchen, who occupied all of northern China. The Song sought refuge at Hangzhou south of the Yangtze River. From this time onward, the dynasty was called the Southern Song and it lasted from 1127–1279 C.E.

Agricultural Revolution

One important development in Song society was the expansion of food production. Rice growing increased in the Yangtze River area as more advanced tools and techniques were used. After 1012 C.E., varieties of rice that mature in early winter were imported from Vietnam. This made two harvests a year possible, and doubled the capacity of the cultivated land. The increase in efficiency of agricultural production freed people from spending so much time working the land, which lead to overall economic expansion and the development of trade. More ceramics were produced with kilns and workshops in many areas. The growth of trade meant that products circulated on a vast scale around the empire. China made full use of extensive networks of waterways from the Yangtze River up to northern China to transport goods. A significant reason for the economic growth was that luxury items were no longer restricted to aristocrats and the imperial family, but a new urban class of wealthy landowners and merchants could also afford them. China exported many luxury goods abroad.

Geographically, the southern Song were restricted to southern China, and had lost access to the trade routes of Central Asia, so they expanded their maritime trade routes. These routes had existed for more than a thousand years, but at this time seafaring activity increased in the ports along the eastern and southern coasts of Fujian, Zhejiang (*Jeh-jee'ang*), and Guangdong. A large Chinese ship that could sail on the open sea, known as a junk, appeared in the tenth to eleventh centuries. These ships could carry as many as 1,000 men and had up to twelve enormous sails. China now looked to the outside world from its southeastern coasts as the Song increased its maritime trade with countries in Southeast Asia.

The Yuan Dynasty (1279–1368 C.E.)

During the thirteenth century the Mongols expanded out of their homeland in the steppe to the north of China and conquered all of East and Central Asia, reaching as far as present-day Hungary in eastern Europe. The eastern part of the Mongol Empire was called the Empire of the Great Khan, or Yuan in Chinese, and engulfed all of China and its neighbors. Although the Mongols only ruled China for 100 years, they opened China further to the influence of peoples from the steppe and Central Asia, and from even as far away as Europe.

Beginning in 1211 C.E. the Mongols began to attack northern China, and by 1234 C.E., they had conquered all of northern China, including the Liao and Tangut peoples. Over the following forty years they managed to gain control of the south of China as well. With little experience of administrating large populations of settled peoples, the Mongols copied Chinese institutions and employed the services of experienced foreign administrators from Central Asia, the Middle East, or Europe. Under these foreign administrators, a postal service began in 1229 C.E., a tax system was set up, and public granaries were built. In 1236 C.E. the first paper money was issued under the Mongols. A translation office was set up to translate the Chinese classics into Mongolian. The first civil service recruitment examinations began in 1237 C.E., and an imperial library was established in the capital Dadu (on the site of present-day Beijing) the following year.

The Mongols classified the population of East Asia into three categories: Mongols; various peoples that were neither

Rich families had estates in the countryside and employed farmers to work the land. This Song Dynasty (960–1279 C.E.) painting shows daily life on the estate of an official or merchant.

500 C.E.		750 C.E.	
Period of Disunity	**Sui Dynasty 589–618 C.E.**	**Tang Dynasty 618–907 C.E.**	

1250 c.e.		1500 c.e.
Song Dynasty 960–1279 c.e.	Yuan Dynasty 1279–1368 c.e.	Ming Dynasty 1368–1644 c.e.

Mongols nor Chinese and had not come under Chinese influence; and Chinese. People were not allowed to marry outside their ethnic classification. Only a Mongolian or a non-Chinese foreigner could occupy important government posts. Deputy governors were usually Muslims. China enjoyed a period of economic expansion during this period, but the Mongols favored trade with non-Chinese peoples of Central Asia, which drained all the profits out of China. The maritime trade continued, though, and Chinese merchants went to live in southeastern Asia, and Mongolian expeditions of Chinese soldiers were sent to Vietnam, Cambodia, Burma, and Java.

The Mongol Yuan Dynasty collapsed for many reasons, not least because it had grown too large to administer, but also because of growing corruption. The use of paper money led to inflation, in which the price of everyday goods increases dramatically as the currency becomes worth less. This led to increasing poverty among the peasants. Large rebellions of peasant, and later local landowners, in Shandong province in eastern China and around the Yangtze River basin, were frequent beginning in 1300 C.E. By the early fourteenth century, the central government was also being weakened by disputes over succession.

Marco Polo

Marco Polo, born in Venice, Italy in 1254 C.E., was a traveler and merchant. Marco's father had already visited the court of the Mongolian ruler, Kublai Khan (1215–1294 C.E.). On his second journey from Venice to China, he took his teenage son Marco with him.

Marco Polo is famous for being one of the first people to journey to China from Europe. He wrote a book about his experiences of traveling from Venice along the Silk Road to China during the Yuan Dynasty (1279–1368 C.E.), which was ruled by Kublai Khan from 1271–1294 C.E. Marco's book is typical of the travel writing of his time and includes many personal stories and reflections, but leaves out much detail about the places he visited. This has caused some historians to doubt whether he really went as far as China, or whether he even left Venice at

Horses were vital to the Mongolians in their military campaigns. This Yuan Dynasty (1279–1368 C.E.) painting shows horses feeding.

Foreigners in China

Various Europeans traveled to the Mongolian Empire as missionaries. They met merchants and administrators from all over Asia. Such foreigners left traces of their influence in China in the form of tombstones and inscriptions in many languages such as Arabic, Syriac, and Tamil. One famous traveler was Ibn Battuta (1304–1377 C.E.) from Tangiers in North Africa. He traveled all over East Asia and spent time in China. His memoirs provide much useful information, for example on the use of water-powered machines in ancient China.

If Mongol domination had lasted longer, this foreign influence would have left a more enduring impact. During the Mongol period, the Chinese also traveled west to the Middle East and may have reached as far as Europe. Mongol rulers favored the spread of Islam in China, and mosques were built in northern China as well as in Guangzhou in the south. But the Mongols also allowed other religions, such as Buddhism, to be practiced.

During the Yuan Dynasty (1279–1368 C.E.), many Muslims came to settle in China as the Mongols accorded them higher status than the Han Chinese. This picture shows the Great Mosque in Xi'an, founded in the Tang Dynasty (618–907 C.E.).

Kublai Khan would listen to accounts of foreign countries, peoples, and religions with great interest. Discussions on a range of topics could be heard at the Khan's court. This scene at court shows Kublai Khan welcoming Marco Polo and his father.

Kublai Khan would sit on a throne on a raised platform. He holds his hand out here in a gesture of benevolence and openness to the guests from a foreign land.

This court lady is playing a two-stringed instrument called an erhu.

At banquets, the Khan would drink out of bowls of pure gold like these.

all, but rather invented his story using information from other books and the accounts of travelers that he met. Other historians are certain that he did reach Mongolian-ruled China. Marco is thought by some to have brought the recipes for ice cream and spaghetti (noodles) back to Italy from China.

In the summer of 1275, Marco Polo and his father arrived at the summer palace of Kublai Khan in Shangdu, north of the Mongol capital Dadu (modern-day Beijing). Kublai had been familiar with Chinese culture from a young age, and surrounded himself with Chinese, Persian, Tibetan, and Turkic Uighur advisors and scholars at court. He was interested in foreign cultures and would listen to new ideas with an open mind. The Polos were well received in the court of Kublai, who was impressed by young Marco. Kublai Khan sent Marco on various missions around his empire to gather information. Marco carried out these missions well and provided Kublai with useful intelligence on the regions he had visited.

After seventeen years of serving Kublai Khan, the Polos were eager to return home. They accompanied a Mongol princess to Persia by sea, and from there traveled back to Venice by land and sea. Soon after their return, Marco was captured by the Genoese after a sea battle between the Italian city-states of Genoa and Venice. He wrote a book of his travels in jail with the help of another prisoner, a writer named Rustichello da Pisa.

The Polos bow down in respect before the Khan.

Although Marco's father had seen the Khan before, it was important for the young Marco to make a good first impression.

Chapter Three

The Power of the Emperor

Chinese emperors were said to rule under the "Mandate of Heaven." This mandate, or command, was the bond thought to exist between the emperor and the "natural world" (heaven), which gave him the right to rule. For example, the emperor would perform rituals in the spring each year to assure a good harvest, and would be blamed if the harvest failed. If he offended the natural world by treating his people badly or failing to provide for them, he would lose the mandate and right to rule over them. This idea appeared in China for the first time during the Zhou Dynasty (c. 1050–221 B.C.E.), and remained influential for nearly 3,000 years up to the reign of the last emperor. Zhou historians used this idea to justify their overthrow of the Shang Dynasty (c. 1600–1050 B.C.E.), saying that the Shang had lost the Mandate of Heaven.

In ancient China, emperors had total power. Emperors usually chose their successors, appointed all officials, and were in charge of the army. The emperor made decisions on whether to order the execution of criminals. He was regarded as a "fountain of justice," and his power was only limited by well established traditions. If emperors were corrupt or tyrannical, they would lose the Mandate of Heaven, and could be overthrown. Beneath the emperor, power was sometimes held by ministers, government officials, or concubines.

Public opinion could be expressed through the advice of counselors and secretaries. The emperor would try to follow public opinion where possible. A group of officials called the Court of Censors informed the emperor on important matters of public welfare, and could criticize anyone, including the emperor, for failing to act lawfully and morally.

This painting shows the Second Qin Emperor riding in a palanquin, a covered box carried on long poles, guarded by a group of soldiers.

Empresses

Nearly all emperors of China were men, yet women often exerted considerable influence at court, and one woman even became empress herself. Toward the end of the Han Dynasty (206 B.C.E.–220 C.E.), after the capital moved from Chang'an to Luoyang, empresses at court managed to take control from weak emperors.

Later, in the Tang Dynasty (618–907 C.E.), Wu Zetian, the wife of Emperor Gaozong, finally became empress in her own right after ruling in his place for many years while he was ill. Empress Wu forged a Buddhist text to justify her ending the Tang and starting a new dynasty in 690 C.E. The story told that Maitreya, the Buddha of the future, would be reborn as a woman, become empress, and bring great prosperity to her people. Many famous and talented officials of the time suggested that Empress Wu was this woman. In 705 C.E. she was removed from the throne, however, and the Tang Dynasty was restored.

Empress Wu (625–705 c.e.) was the only woman to rule China in all its history.

Great Emperors: Wu Di and Xuanzong

Wu Di was one of the great emperors of the Han Dynasty (206 B.C.E.–220 C.E.) and ruled from 141–87 B.C.E. He was given the name Wu Di, which means "the warlike emperor," after he conquered large amounts of territory beyond the Han homeland. He adopted the teachings of Confucius as state philosophy and code of morals, and opened schools to teach officials the classic books of Confucius.

In 129 B.C.E., Wu Di sent four generals with 10,000 troops each to fight the Xiongnu after they had attacked a Chinese position. One general captured the Xiongnu city of Shuofang in 127 B.C.E., which then became a staging post for the Han to make military expeditions into Central Asia.

Wu Di's reign lasted fifty-four years, which was the longest reign of an emperor until Kangxi (*Kang-she*) (1661–1722 C.E.) during the Qing (*Ching*) Dynasty (1644–1911 C.E.).

Zhang Qian: Wu Di's Ambassador

In 139 B.C.E. Emperor Wu Di asked General Zhang Qian (*Jang-Chee'en*) to go to regions west of Han China to the lands of the Yuezhi (*Yoo'eh-jrih*) to form an alliance against the Xiongnu, a people from the steppe to the northwest of China who controlled the routes west out of China. Zhang Qian was immediately captured by the Xiongnu and lived with them for ten years, taking a Xiongnu wife.

After spending a decade in captivity, Zhang Qian escaped from his captors and arrived in present-day northern Afghanistan, where the Yuezhi had relocated, only to be taken prisoner again by the Xiongnu on his return. Zhang Qian eventually escaped again and arrived back in Chang'an in 126 B.C.E. After thirteen years living in Central Asia, Zhang Qian was able to provide valuable information to Emperor Wu Di about the outside world. With Qian's help—along with a strong military—Wu Di extended Han Chinese influence to Xiongnu lands as far as Ferghana in Central Asia, including Korea in the northeast, and Vietnam in the south.

Zhang Qian opened up the outside world to the Chinese, which resulted in an influx of goods and ideas from other countries. This statue of Zhang Qian is near Dunhuang in northwest China, from where he would have traveled toward the western regions of Central Asia.

Yang Guifei was the favorite concubine of the Tang Emperor Xuanzong. She is renowned in Chinese history for her beauty. This painting shows her mounting a horse. Her life ended in tragedy as the emperor was forced to put her to death during the An Lushan rebellion.

Civil Service Examinations

During the Han Dynasty (206 B.C.E.–220 C.E.) officials were usually appointed by recommendations of other senior officials and aristocrats. In the Sui Dynasty (589–618 C.E.), the first written examinations were introduced to recruit candidates to serve in the civil service bureaucracy. These continued during the Tang Dynasty (618–907 C.E.), when rulers gradually used the written examinations to recruit officials by ability rather than by recommendations. Subjects examined during the Tang included the knowledge of the classics, law, history, mathematics, and military ability, including tests of shooting and physical strength. The most popular and important competition was an examination in general knowledge and literary skills, including the ability to write poetry. Candidates had to memorize long, complicated texts which they analyzed with written essays.

A hopeful candidate for the civil service respectfully hands in his script to the emperor. Competition was extremely tough.

Tang Xuanzong (685–762 C.E.)

Emperor Xuanzong's reign lasted from 712–756 C.E., which was forty-four years, the longest of any emperor of the Tang Dynasty (618–907 C.E.). Under his rule the Tang made many great achievements. As well as fighting state corruption and improving the economy, Xuanzong had many endearing personal qualities. His reign saw only a small number of executions carried out compared to other periods in Chinese history. Other examples of his generous policies include redistributing land from government offices to the poor and giving tax relief to the poorest families in each village throughout the empire. He also improved the education and health systems.

Xuanzong was a great supporter of the arts. He himself was an accomplished musician, calligrapher, and poet. He could play the Central Asian drum, and his tastes included both Chinese and foreign music.

Keeping Officials in Line

During the Song Dynasty (960–1279 C.E.), officials did not spend all their time in active service. High officials were sometimes given honorary positions as custodians of Buddhist and Daoist temples. Eventually, any official could apply for these "empty" positions like any other commission. Each assignment or commission only lasted for three or four years, and officials could not be reassigned to the same post without special permission from the emperor. Officials also had to obey the "law of avoidance," which meant they could not serve in their hometowns, areas where they owned large amounts of property, or localities where close relatives held office. This prevented officials from becoming too powerful and corrupt.

This sculpture dates from the Tang Dynasty and depicts a government official wearing a traditional hat or headscarf.

A Civil Service Career: Su Shi

Su Shi (1037–1101 C.E.) was a poet, calligrapher, and painter, and also served as an official. He was typical of his time in that he combined a public career in government with artistic talent. Like many other lively, able scholar-officials in Chinese history, he often got into trouble, and ended up being sent into exile away from the court several times. He wrote an essay voicing his concern that the Board of Policy Criticism, through which popular opinion was expressed to the emperor, was being threatened. Su Shi saw this government department as very important for officials to voice their opinions on matters of state. He wrote: *"Once the channel for public criticism has been closed, not even the greatest hero will be able to rise.... A time will come when the emperor will stand alone, the system will disintegrate, and anything could happen."*

Su Shi wrote at length about his experiences when he was away from the capital. This stone sculpture of Su Shi can be seen at Meishan, in southwest China's Sichuan province.

He established a group called the Pear Garden Troupe that trained musicians and experimented with new music. Xuanzong left a mixed legacy, however, because in his old age he became obsessed with one of his son's wives, Yang Guifei. His reign ended with the An Lushan Rebellion of 755 C.E. and he was forced into exile, where he reluctantly had Yang Guifei put to death and abdicated.

Civil Service

The state bureaucracy in China can trace its roots back more than 2,000 years to when China was united for the first time under the Qin Dynasty (221–206 B.C.E.). The huge expanse of territory of the united empire meant that the new government needed a way of managing the different tasks involved in ruling the people. The large system of government officials ruling all levels of society throughout the empire was called a bureaucracy. Today we tend to think of bureaucracy in a negative sense as a heavy-handed system of unnecessary procedures, but it was an effective way of running a large, complex empire like ancient China.

From the reign of First Emperor Qin (259–210 B.C.E.) in the third century B.C.E. until modern times, the state bureaucracy controlled most fields of activity in China. The best career for an ambitious man was therefore to work for the government as a civil servant, rather than join the army.

As China's population grew during the Song Dynasty (960–1279 C.E.), the civil service had to be developed and expanded to recruit talented men to administer the empire. Later reforms in the Song created three different levels of exams, with competitions in the prefectures, in the capital, and in the palace in the presence of the emperor. Eventually only one kind of competition was used, and exam papers were kept anonymous to guarantee that candidates were treated fairly. Success in these exams was not always enough, however, to guarantee advancement, and candidates also needed a recommendation to be promoted.

Because of the development that took place from the eleventh to thirteenth centuries, the civil service became more important in the political system. This gave the scholar-officials the

Dongpo Pork

Su Shi famously wrote a memorial (a written communication) to the emperor, criticizing the social reforms of Wang Anshi. As a result of his direct opposition to the new laws, he was sent far away from court to live in exile. During his time in exile, he acquired a new name, Su Dongpo. "Su" was his family name, and "Dongpo" meant "the eastern slope." This referred to the hill where he now lived. One day he began to cook some pork for lunch when a friend came to visit him. Su Shi became distracted and forgot about the pork, until a fragrant smell coming from the kitchen reminded him. Ever since, a Chinese dish of slow-cooked pork has been named "Dongpo pork" after him.

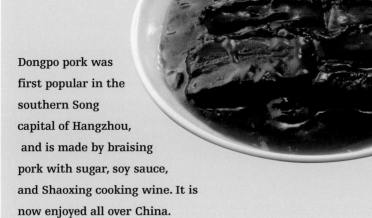

Dongpo pork was first popular in the southern Song capital of Hangzhou, and is made by braising pork with sugar, soy sauce, and Shaoxing cooking wine. It is now enjoyed all over China.

greatest amount of power they had ever enjoyed in Chinese history. Other individuals, such as favorites or members of the royal court, had little influence over state affairs during this period. In addition, the eleventh century saw the formation of political parties with different opinions, which often led to bitter conflicts. Positions were divided into *jinmin* (near the people) and non-*jinmin* positions. Positions "not near the people" were mainly concerned with administrating state business operations. Ambitious officials would try to get *jinmin* positions, which included general administration and governance of the people.

Law and Order

China has a long legal tradition that draws mainly from two branches: Confucianism and Legalism. For most of its history, law in China has been based on Confucian philosophy and the idea of social control through moral education. It has also used the Legalist tradition of codified law and punishment.

The word for law in ancient China was *fa*, which meant "fair," "straight," and "just." Law was kept separate from religion in China, and some saw the need for laws as evidence of a moral decline in society. At first, there was no formal system of laws. Instead people accepted ethical norms more through customs and moral values engrained into them from an early age.

The Confucian tradition maintained that human behavior should be regulated through education. The concept of *li* (moral propriety or natural law) came from human feelings about the right thing to do. Thus "law" could be used in conjunction with *li* as a system of rewards and

Showing obedience to elders was important in families and across society in ancient China. In this twelfth-century painting, a disobedient young man is brought before a judge.

penalties to encourage people to behave well. The ideal ruler would be benevolent and the ideal subject loyal. Confucius taught that *li* is in harmony with universal reason and eternal principles. *Li* should therefore conform to human feeling and universal reason.

The Legalists preferred to govern society through law rather than through *li* (a natural sense of what was right). They wanted the law to be made public to both subjects and ruler, and applied equally to all, no matter what the relationship. They believed that *fa* needed to be severe in its punishment in order to be effective. This was founded on the Legalist concept that human nature is basically evil, an idea they inherited from the philosopher Xunzi (*Shoo'un-tzuh*), who lived and worked around 298–238 B.C.E.

Both Confucians and Legalists agreed, however, that the emperor had absolute power over all aspects of life, including law. The Legalist tradition laid the main foundations of the legal system. The Han Dynasty (206 B.C.E.–220 C.E.) kept the legal system inherited from the Qin Dynasty (221–206 B.C.E.) but modified some of its harsher aspects with Confucian notions of social controls. The Han Dynasty recognized four sources of law: codified laws, orders from the emperor, laws inherited from previous dynasties, and previous cases. Orders from the emperor commanded the greatest power out of all of these. During the reign of Emperor Wu Di, Confucianism was given authority as the official doctrine and other systems of thought were banned.

The *Liji* (Classic of Rites) says, "to rule a state without using *li* is as impossible as plowing a field without a plow." Han Feizi, a Legalist, wrote, "Law is decreed by the government, and learned by the people. Violation of the law will be punished and obedience of the law will be rewarded."

Confucius (traditionally 551–479 B.C.E.) never lived to see his philosophy become influential in Chinese government and society. His ideas are becoming popular again in China today.

200 B.C.E	300 C.E.	
Han Dynasty 206 B.C.E.–220 C.E.		Period of Disunity
Zhang Qian 195–114 B.C.E.	Wu Di 141–87 B.C.E.	

The Tang Code of Law

The Tang Code of law was influenced by the Confucian moral system. Criminal acts committed by senior family members against junior ones went unpunished or slightly punished, whereas the same offense by a junior member against a senior member received more severe punishment. The Tang Code was first issued in 624 C.E. and finalized in 637 C.E. It had an important influence on later dynasties in Chinese history and on other countries in East Asia, such as Japan. The Code lent stability to the state since threats to the country were severely punished. The severity of punishments depended on the relationship of the criminal to the victim. The magistrate would decide the precise nature of the offense from the models described in the Code.

Buddhists in China believed in Hell and being judged after death for their actions in this life. This painting shows people receiving punishments in Hell before they pass to another life.

	800 C.E.			1200 C.E.
Sui Dynasty 589–618 C.E.	Tang Dynasty 618–907 C.E.		Song Dynasty 960–1279 C.E.	
	Wu Zetian 625–705 C.E.	Xuanzong 712–756 C.E.	Su Shi 1037–1101 C.E.	

Chapter Four

Going to War

The Chinese Army

During the Shang and Zhou Dynasties, which extended from about 1600 to 221 B.C.E., Chinese armies were formed of infantry, or foot soldiers, and war chariots. Each chariot had two spoked wheels and was commanded by an archer. During the Western Zhou Dynasty (1050–771 B.C.E.), the king was said to control six armies of chariots. He also gave territories to his feudal lords to rule and protect.

During the Spring and Autumn Period (770–476 B.C.E.) rituals were performed before an attack, and the enemy was given time to prepare before battle. After this, during the Warring States Period (475–221 B.C.E.), new military tactics replaced chariot warfare with cavalry charges, and ritual was replaced by deception and ruthless strategy. The pastoral peoples living to the north and northeast of China in the first millennium B.C.E. probably adopted horseback riding, but most of the Chinese army of this period was composed of foot soldiers equipped with iron swords, iron-tipped spears, and crossbows.

As its name suggests, the scale of armed conflict increased dramatically in the Warring States Period, and most men had to spend some time serving in the army. In 307 B.C.E., to make fighting and riding on horseback easier, King Wuling of Zhao ordered his troops to wear clothing in the style of nomadic peoples, including trousers and shorter tunics with split sides and tight sleeves instead of flowing robes.

Dunhuang and the surrounding area were conquered by the Tibetans from 781 C.E. to 848 C.E. This wall painting from the Mogao caves at Dunhuang shows soldiers commanded by Zhang Yichao, who drove the Tibetans out of Dunhuang and swore allegiance to the emperor.

Committing Troops to Battle

To keep the power of the military under control, the Qin and Han dynasties devised a system where bronze tiger figurines were divided in half. An army commander or local official kept one half. The government in the capital kept the other half. Troops could only be sent to battle when the other matching half was presented to their commander.

Before the sixth century B.C.E., armies were composed of a few thousand men, and it is recorded that many battles were resolved in one day of fighting. By the end of the third century B.C.E., the large states would assemble armies of tens of thousands men and wars could last for years. Armies could fight each other for several months.

During the Han Dynasty (206 B.C.E.–220 C.E.), men were drafted to the army for two years. A small number served in the capital, but the majority was sent to man the walled defenses along the northern frontier. Under the Sui Dynasty (589–618 C.E.) and Tang Dynasty (618–907 C.E.), land was given to farmers in return for their services as soldiers. Most of these "soldier-farmer" military units were situated in the northwest. This system declined under Empress Wu (625–705 C.E.), and was replaced by a standing army under Emperor Xuanzong (685–762 C.E.) in the northwest. The army's Chinese troops included many men displaced by economic changes made by the Tang. Non-Chinese men such as Koreans, Khitans, Turks, and Sogdians also served in the armies.

There was no central army to resist the An Lushan rebellion in 755 C.E., so the Chinese had to recruit the help of the Turkic Uighur soldiers. This meant the Chinese had to pay them heavy compensation. After this period, Tang emperors recognized the need for a central army as a counterweight to the regional warlords.

During the early Song Dynasty (960–1279 C.E.), the army was able to reunite the southern states. But it was not strong enough to destroy the two states ruled by Central Asian peoples, the Tangut Xixia (*She-shee'ah*) to the northwest and the Khitan Liao to the northeast. The central army became larger and more expensive while soldiers became poorer and less capable. Thus a northern people called the Jurchen (*Jer-chen*) were able to conquer Kaifeng (*Kai-fung*) and the rest of north China quite easily. A popular saying in the Song Dynasty reflected society's attitude to the army: "Good iron is not made into nails, nor are good men made into soldiers."

After his conquest of China in the thirteenth century, Genghis Khan organized his Mongolian population according to tribal military units. Each warrior was assigned a unit with his family and possessions and would be executed if he tried to leave it unlawfully.

Weapons and Armor

In ancient China, armor was designed specifically for the different roles of each type of soldier. Charioteers, who did not move once they were driving their chariots, wore long, heavy armor that protected their entire body, while leaving their arms free to move. The infantry, who needed to move quickly on the ground to be effective, wore shorter leather suits that were much lighter. The cavalry could have heavier armor but they needed light protection on their legs in order to be free to ride, and so wore leggings in the style of peoples from the steppe.

Armor in the early Shang Dynasty (c. 1600–1050 B.C.E.) was made from turtle shells tied together with cord. Bronze and leather were used in later periods. Armor was decorated and often very heavy. Shang warriors wore armor made from leather that covered the front and back of their bodies, and bronze helmets to protect their heads.

During the Zhou Dynasty (1050–221 B.C.E.) some new styles of armor were introduced. One was called *gejia (Geh-jee'ah)*. This was a sleeveless suit of animal hide attached to pieces of wood. Buffalo and rhinoceros hide was often used. During the Zhou period, armor was produced by attaching boiled leather to a fabric backing, then applying many layers of red lacquer, or paint. When used together with a large shield, this armor could protect soldiers against the bronze weapons of the period. Leather armor was also sometimes reinforced by a bronze plate worn over the chest.

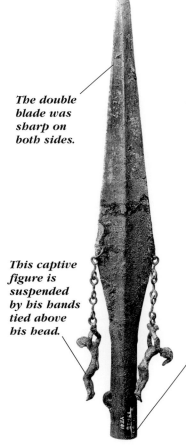

The double blade was sharp on both sides.

This captive figure is suspended by his hands tied above his head.

The base of the spear is thick to provide a good grip for the shaft.

The size of armies increased dramatically during the Warring States Period (475–221 B.C.E.). This made it impossible to provide armor for every soldier, and only the higher-ranking soldiers wore it. For protection, infantrymen would wear armor made of several small overlapping metal or leather plates laced together, along with shoulder guards and helmets.

Long spears, or *qiang (Chi-ang)*, were the most popular long weapons in ancient China, and were known as the "King of Weapons." This Han Dynasty spear is decorated with two prisoners dangling on chains.

A Soldier of the Warring States Period

Warfare became more frequent and sophisticated during the Warring States Period (475–221 B.C.E.). Iron and cavalry were used in warfare for the first time, and armies were now formed of several thousand men. Larger numbers of foot soldiers such as this one were often decisive in winning battles.

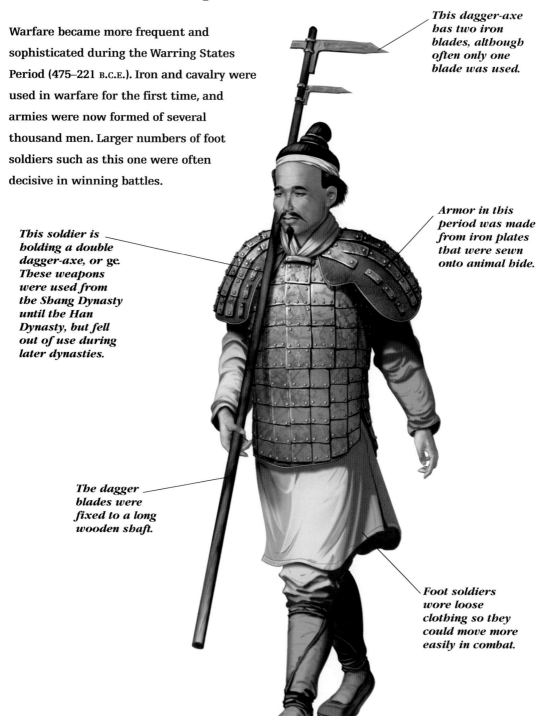

This dagger-axe has two iron blades, although often only one blade was used.

Armor in this period was made from iron plates that were sewn onto animal hide.

This soldier is holding a double dagger-axe, or ge. These weapons were used from the Shang Dynasty until the Han Dynasty, but fell out of use during later dynasties.

The dagger blades were fixed to a long wooden shaft.

Foot soldiers wore loose clothing so they could move more easily in combat.

Chinese Military Strategy

The continual warfare during the Warring States Period (475–221 B.C.E.) meant rulers and military commanders had to continually develop clever ways of achieving victory at the least cost. Many books were written on military strategy during this period. A famous example is the *Art of War* by Sunzi (*Sun-zuh*), which is still read by people around the world today.

Sunzi's strategy was to manipulate the enemy for an easy victory. The highest goal was to conquer other states without ever having to fight them. He advised using both "orthodox" and "unorthodox" ways to achieve victory. Orthodox ways referred to the conventional warfare of frontal attack with great strength. Unorthodox ways referred to using flexible forces in imaginative, unconventional ways such as circular or "flanking" side attacks. Speed and surprise were also important elements for winning a battle. Therefore absolute self-control was essential. Sunzi says, "He who knows both the enemy and himself will not face danger in a hundred battles. He who does not know the enemy but knows himself will sometimes win battles, sometimes lose. He who knows neither the enemy nor himself will usually face defeat in every battle."

By the time of the Han Dynasty (206 B.C.E.–220 C.E.), enough armor was made to supply large armies of hundreds of thousands of soldiers. Better protection was needed from the crossbows and iron swords now used in battle, so armor began to be made from iron. Under the rule of the Han, horses wore armor too. Cavalry came to play an increasingly important role in battles. The rigid stirrup came into use by the fourth to fifth centuries C.E., which made the cavalry more effective by allowing the rider more stability and freedom of movement.

The sword did not develop fully in China until the late Spring and Autumn Period (770–476 B.C.E.). Before this, soldiers used daggers, spears, or short swords, which were all made from bronze. Early swords were designed for piercing and thrusting, not for full-frontal attacks. By the time of the early Han, armies began to use a sword with a pointed, double-edged blade called a *jian* (*Jee'an*).

This bronze sword was excavated in central China's Hubei province. The inscription on the blade reads, "Belonging to King Goujian of Yue, made for his personal use."

As cavalry featured more and more prominently in combat, the sword developed for use on horseback. During the Han Dynasty, a single-edged sword with a ring handle replaced the long sword of the Warring States Period (475–221 B.C.E.). Weapons were either both short and functional for use in battle, or beautifully decorated and used purely in ceremonies. Until the time of the Song Dynasty (960–1279 C.E.), armies were composed of cavalry, consisting of mounted archers and armored lancers, supported by infantry armed with spears, swords, and bows.

The Battle of Changping, 260 B.C.E.

The Battle of Changping was one of the deadliest fought by the armies of the state of Qin in their quest to unite China. The Qin invaded the state of Han in 265 B.C.E. and brought most of the territory under its control. There was one province, Shangdang, that was cut off from most of the Han state, however, and had not been conquered. In desperation the Han state gave the province to the neighboring Zhao kingdom. The Zhao king accepted the land and sent Lian Po (*Li'en-paw*) to lead an army against the Qin. The Qin were eager to take Shangdang now because it would leave the Zhao kingdom open to attack.

Lian Po decided to build defenses against the Qin. He built several fortresses in 260 B.C.E. and waited for the invading army to leave. A stalemate of three months followed where nothing happened. The Qin sent spies to Zhao and Han spreading rumors that Lian Po was old and unable to command his army. The king of Zhao then replaced him with another general named Zhao Kuo. The Qin also put a new, better commander in charge of their army.

When Zhao Kuo took command in 260 B.C.E., the Zhao army had 400,000 men. He ordered his troops to attack the Qin camp. The Qin pretended to flee, but left 25,000 troops waiting in ambush to block the Zhao army from retreating. The Zhao charged as far as the Qin fortress, but the Qin troops ambushed the rear of the Zhao. Five thousand Qin cavalry took the Zhao fortress. The Zhao troops were now split in two, and could not attack further or retreat. All they could do was build defenses on a hill and wait for reinforcements.

The Zhao troops were besieged for forty-six days. Driven to desperation by hunger and thirst, Zhao Kuo and some of his men charged down the hill, but were shot down by Qin archers. The rest of the Zhao army surrendered. The Qin commander had them all executed to prevent further rebellion. The state of Zhao was greatly weakened by the battle, and was finally captured by the Qin thirty years later.

The Great Wall of China

The Great Wall of China that we can see today dates from the Ming Dynasty (1368–1644 C.E.), although it was repaired extensively in the twentieth century. There was never one single Great Wall, but a series of walls built in different places and at different times in Chinese history. Such walls were constructed as part of military strategy, for enclosing territory and claiming land far into the steppe and desert of northwestern China. They were also built as a defense against marauding northern tribes, but walls did not usually stop invasions into China. Dynasties that had the most military success, such as the Tang (618–907 C.E.) and Yuan (1279–1368 C.E.) did not build walls, but instead used superior military tactics. The walls were

Horses in battle would wear protective armor. These figurines from the early sixth century include military attendants on armored horses and mounted drummers. The drummers would perform military music during a battle.

Observation towers were built within sight of each other to send signals along the wall.

Towers and forts were used for observation, communication, defense, and shelter.

Archers would take up positions on the wall to fire on enemy forces.

Men worked on bamboo scaffolding to position the bricks.

also used for regulating trade as a customs barrier. However, the officials who manned them were easily bribed and would often let invaders pass through.

During the Zhou Dynasty (1050–221 B.C.E.), Chinese states had to adapt to the cultural style and military challenges of their northern neighbors in order to survive. For example, swift mounted archers soon replaced the traditional Zhou chariots. Many Chinese states began building walls both against the northern tribes and each other, starting in the seventh century B.C.E. and onward. The Qin, Yao, and Zhao states all built walls along the northern frontier around the end of the fourth century B.C.E.

The earliest walls in the second and third millennia B.C.E. were made from compacted dirt. These walls followed the natural contours of the land. Where the land was flatter, ramparts

The Great Wall is a powerful symbol of China, and shows how China has been influenced by the outside world throughout its history. It is composed of a number of individual fortifications built in different styles and materials used at different times.

Local soil could be dug up and fired into bricks.

Men would often carry heavy bricks on barrows over difficult terrain.

Officials supervised the building work.

were constructed of stamped dirt and stones. The border regions defined by these walls became areas of conflict over the next 2,000 years.

The wall of the Qin Dynasty (221–206 B.C.E.) was probably made of stamped dirt like the walls built during the Warring States Period (475–221 B.C.E.), and it is likely that the Qin wall was built on the foundations of older walls. A Chinese folk name for ancient northern walls was "earth dragon." Slaves, soldiers, and peasants were forced to build the wall, and many people lost their lives in the harsh, remote conditions. Some of those who died were buried in the walls.

During the Han Dynasty (206 B.C.E.–220 C.E.), the Qin system of walls was repaired and extended further. A wall dating from the Han Dynasty was discovered in the early twentieth century near Dunhuang in the desert in western China. It was made by compressing layers of the local dirt, clay, or gravel, into bundles of twigs or reeds. The Han wall at Dunhuang was 8 feet (2.5 meters) thick, and almost 6 feet 6 inches (2 meters) high, and 60 miles (96 kilometers) long. There were also watchtowers along the wall, where objects from everyday life used during the Han Dynasty were found. The towers also contained many thin strips of wood on which details of grain supply, the postal system, and customs taxes were written. These walls were part of a broader military strategy that included many different elements, such as forging alliances with neighboring tribes, using army outposts, and breeding horses for the military.

The Mongolian troops of Genghis Khan (1162–1227 C.E.) went around the defensive walls, or were allowed to gain entry through passes by corrupt generals. By 1217 C.E. Genghis Khan had occupied all of China north of the Yellow River, and later went on to take the whole country.

Inventions for War: Gunpowder and the Crossbow

Gunpowder was invented in China during the Tang Dynasty (618–907 C.E.) after many centuries of experiments with chemicals. In ancient China many scientists practiced chemistry with the aim of making a medicine or potion that would give everlasting life. No such potion was ever found. However, through this process of trial and error they learned how to distill alcohol for drinking, and how to separate salts from alkali metals. One of these salts was saltpeter (potassium nitrate). Further experiments conducted by the Chinese showed that a mixture of sulfur charcoal, and saltpeter exploded after being lit with a flame.

The Great Wall was a series of walls and towers. This ancient beacon tower at Dunhuang in northwest China is about 2,000 years old. Soldiers would have lit fires to send messages to other beacon towers along the wall.

Gunpowder was used in warfare from the early tenth century. It was pounded into balls, which could be thrown from catapults during a siege. These simple bombs were called "flying fires." Gunpowder could also be attached to arrows that would explode on impact, and it was later used to make rockets in bamboo tubes and basic guns. The formula for gunpowder, along with the idea that it could be used as an explosive in a tube, was passed to Europe through the Islamic Middle East in the late thirteenth century.

The crossbow was invented in the fourth century B.C.E. and perfected in the first century B.C.E. The mechanical release of the bow from the crossbow meant that an archer could use a bow which required more force to draw than his natural arm strength, and also meant that he would tire less quickly when firing arrows continuously. The crossbow was important in the battles of the Warring States Period (475 B.C.E.–221 B.C.E.), and required advanced bronze technology to make mechanisms that allowed accurate shots. The crossbow was useful for firing volleys of arrows into a walled city in siege warfare. A soldier would insert his foot into a loop on the crossbow to draw the bow ready to fire. This released the arrow with more force and speed.

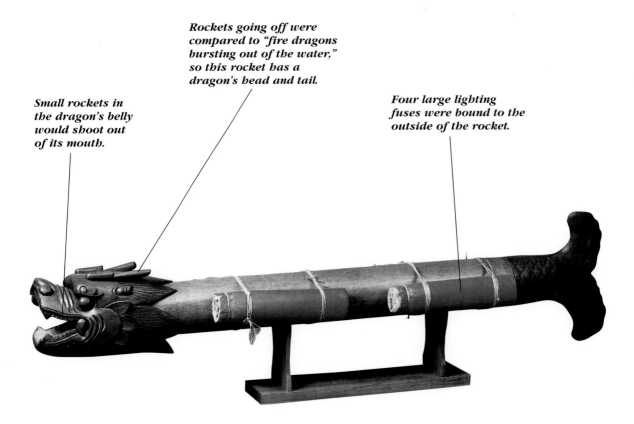

Rockets going off were compared to "fire dragons bursting out of the water," so this rocket has a dragon's head and tail.

Small rockets in the dragon's belly would shoot out of its mouth.

Four large lighting fuses were bound to the outside of the rocket.

The ancient Chinese invented rockets. This rocket was made of wood and bamboo and is the earliest two-stage rocket in the world.

Chinese soldiers had a disciplined method of using the crossbow in battle. They worked in three groups: the back group would load their crossbows, the middle rank would advance ready to shoot, and the front group would shoot their arrows while using shields to protect their flanks. Once they had shot their arrows, they would quickly drop back to the rear to reload.

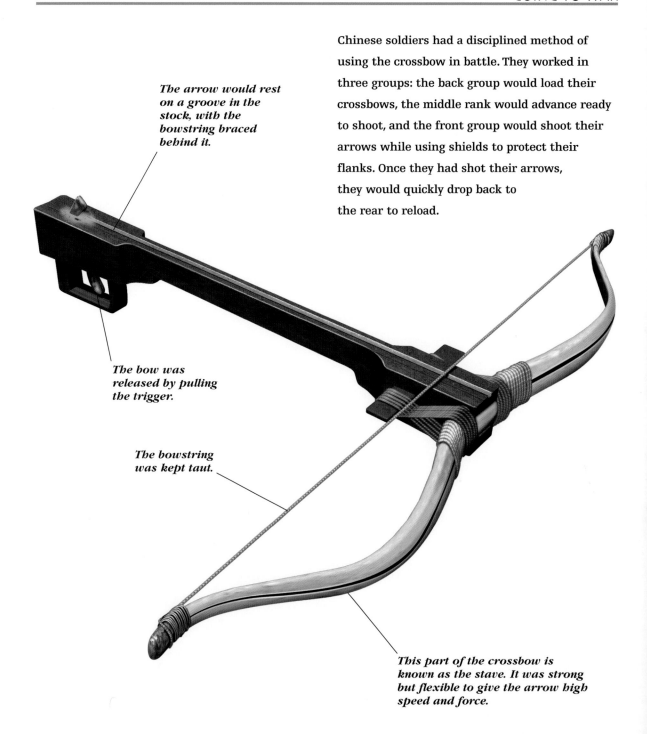

The arrow would rest on a groove in the stock, with the bowstring braced behind it.

The bow was released by pulling the trigger.

The bowstring was kept taut.

This part of the crossbow is known as the stave. It was strong but flexible to give the arrow high speed and force.

Crossbows were still highly regarded during the Song Dynasty (960–1279 C.E.). The *Compilation of Military Classics* of 1044 C.E. states, "The crossbow is the deadliest weapon of China and what the four kinds of barbarians most fear and obey." In battles against foreign cavalry, the crossbowmen would fire first, over the heads of the crouching infantry, who were armed with ordinary bows and pikes.

Chapter Five

Society in Action

Ancient Chinese society divided the people who came under the emperor and aristocrats into four social classes. Scholars were at the top of this social ladder because they could read and write. They were considered the guardians of moral values and knowledge, and were often also government officials. Next came the peasants because they produced wealth for the state from their harvests of crops. Under the peasants came the craftspeople, or artisans, who produced useful goods for daily life as well as beautiful objects. Finally came the merchants at the bottom of society. These groupings should only be seen as broad generalizations, however, since boundaries between them were not always clearly defined, especially after the commercial revolution of the Song Dynasty (960–1279 C.E.). In addition, many social groups were excluded from these categories, such as soldiers, clergy, entertainers, servants, and low-class laborers.

Emperors and Aristocrats

The emperor and his close and extended family were at the top of ancient Chinese society. The emperor's family, the aristocracy, would be given money from the annual tax revenue, and would control estates with the permission of the emperor. During the Han Dynasty (206 B.C.E.–220 C.E.) the status of these aristocratic families came from the lavish lifestyle they were able to afford and the local respect they commanded. They had influence over areas where they owned land, and the largest of these families had hundreds of members. The men were highly educated and had wide cultural interests. By the late Han, with the collapse of the central government, some of these families became powerful at the national level. By the Tang Dynasty (618–907 C.E.), the aristocracy was composed of powerful clans of

Traditional activities of aristocratic women included the making of silk clothes. In this twelfth-century painting, court ladies are pounding silk with poles.

Aristocratic Pastimes

The game of polo, a bit like hockey played on horseback, was introduced to China from India or Central Asia. It was popular with both men and women of the Tang aristocracy. The upper classes welcomed anything "foreign," whether it was dancing, music, games, cooking, clothing fashions, or houses. Some princes and nobles worked as administrators, while others became scholars and gave support to the arts and learning. One prince used his wealth to buy rare books and fine collections of calligraphy and copies of stone inscriptions.

Both men and women played polo in Tang Dynasty China. This painting shows some aristocrats returning after a game of polo.

families who had held high government positions for many generations. Although they would gradually lose their power over the next few hundred years, they continued to lead lavish lifestyles, indulging in hunting, drinking, and various kinds of entertainment.

When the Tang Dynasty was overthrown in the late ninth century and the state bureaucracy collapsed, members of the old aristocratic families lost their center of power. They no longer had bases of local influence and new rulers and bureaucracies had no use for them. This meant that, from then on, advancement in society had to be obtained through the civil service examinations.

Scholars

Scholarship and learning have been respected throughout Chinese history, starting from the Han Dynasty (206 B.C.E.–220 C.E.) and onward, when rulers used the teachings of Confucius as standards for moral behavior in society. One of the most famous sayings of Confucius praises the joy and importance of learning: "To learn, and to put into practice at the right time what one has learned, is that not a pleasure?"

In ancient China, most people could not read or write. Scholars usually came from privileged families who could afford private tutors to teach their sons to read, write, and to memorize important texts. In the Warring States Period (475–221 B.C.E.), gentlemen seeking employment needed skills in *wen*, the literary arts, and in *wu*, the military arts.

During the Han Dynasty the number of scholars serving the emperors increased with the reign of each emperor. These men were well versed in the books of morality, poetry, and history, which were commonly called the Confucian classics. Daoists, diviners, and men familiar with ancient knowledge also continued to advise the Han court. History was written in a precise chronological style recording events by day, month, and year of reign.

During the Period of Disunity that took place between the Han and Tang dynasties in the third to seventh centuries, scholars prized independence of mind and freedom over being

Scholars would often work together editing and compiling texts. This seventh-century painting shows a group of scholars discussing and correcting classical works.

China's First History Book

A historian called Sima Qian wrote a book known as the Historical Records. The book tells the history of China from the earliest times down to Qian's own time, but also includes essays on certain themes, and biographies of famous people. The method of recording history in this book served as a model for all the official histories produced for the next 2,000 years up to modern times.

When Sima Qian was twenty years old, he began a journey through China to collect useful historical records for his work, to verify ancient legends and visit historic sites.

conventional. This stood in direct opposition to the classical moral tradition. During the Tang Dynasty (618–907 C.E.) scholars pursued Buddhist studies to their highest level and wrote some of the finest Chinese poetry. This poetry drew on the rich legacy of classical times as well as absorbing new influences from the steppe and oases of Central Asia and other distant lands. Scholars became more influential in society beginning in the Tang, because men wanting to gain official government posts now had to pass official examinations. To be successful they had to master a vast amount of knowledge and be skilled in writing poetry.

In the Song Dynasty (960–1279 C.E.) printing effected the spread of learning and created a new class of educated people. Changes were taking place in every area of society. Scholars began to test new theories of knowledge through experiments and rational analysis. They devoted themselves purely to learning and did not like to exert themselves physically. Scholars developed wide interests in painting, calligraphy, and collecting fine art, as well as writing. A new type of lyrical poetry that was sung aloud appeared. The scholar-officials acquired even greater political power because of the enhanced importance of the civil service in society.

The Song Dynasty was an age of great intellectual activity, and progress was made in all fields of knowledge, including science and mathematics. Scholars made large collections of texts, and the first encyclopedias and catalogs of books were produced. Private writings, such as diaries and unofficial histories, circulated in greater numbers than ever before. Official historians rediscovered the literary qualities of the great Han historians. A scholar named Zhu Xi (*Joo-she*) revived the classical Confucian tradition by writing commentaries on the classic books of Confucius.

In this way, the advances made in the Song provided the foundations for the development of imperial China up to modern times.

Peasants and Farmers

From its earliest foundations, China has been predominantly an agricultural society. Throughout the period covered in this book, peasants accounted for more than two-thirds of the population. Wealth was created by surpluses from harvests collected by the peasants, and their hard work provided the resources that supported the aristocrats, paid officials, supplied armies, and funded public constructions, such as road and bridge building.

Peasants were so important to the prosperity of the country that they came directly under the scholar-officials in the social pecking order, above the artisans and merchants. In peasant families, men would usually work the land and the women would weave textiles.

In the Tang Dynasty (618–907 c.e.) land was equally distributed to each peasant family to grow enough crops for

This painting shows a variety of everyday activities including farmers hunting and sowing rice in the paddy fields, artisans producing pottery, and women weaving silk.

A Hard Life

Peasants faced many hardships in their daily lives, and would have to work from dawn to dusk every day. They relied on what they grew to survive and could face starvation if their crops were destroyed. Pests such as rats, rabbits, or locusts could strip fields bare. Natural disasters such as floods or heavy rain could ruin crops. To counter these threats, by the time of the Tang Dynasty (618–907 c.e.), the government set up stores of grain called granaries. Local officials could then hand out extra grain for food if disaster struck.

themselves and for paying taxes. The peasant had to pay three taxes in the form of grain, silk, or hemp, and labor on public works. Farmers living in the north could also be called to serve in the army to fight in wars for up to three years. Regular surveys of the peasant population aimed to ensure that farmers were paying all of their taxes. The equal-land system was applied in the dry, wheat-growing areas of northern China. However, it became more difficult to divide land equally in the wetter, rice-growing areas of southern China.

Revolts and Rebellions

Because peasants were known for starting rebellions if conditions became unbearable for them, the rulers of China always tried to ensure that they were kept happy and under control. However, poor Chinese peasants started many of the rebellions against the Mongolian occupiers in the fourteenth century because they were angry at the harsh treatment they received at the hands of the invaders.

Rebellions against imperial power were common in Chinese history. This painting shows the Tang Emperor Xuanzong fleeing with his concubine Yang Guifei after the An Lushan Rebellion in 755 C.E.

By the Song Dynasty (960–1279 C.E.) an increase in population meant that peasants were divided into landowners and those who did not own any land. Farmers who owned the most land would also enforce order and act as a local police force. Peasants who did not own land were very poor and were paid little for their labor, and if their situation became really bad they would rebel. Otherwise the expanded economy provided them with other chances of employment, such as joining the army or working in large-scale workshops as craftsmen. Farmers also found work in the cities as store clerks, waiters, or servants in the mansions of rich families and merchants.

Artists and Craftspeople

Up to the time of the Han Dynasty (206 B.C.E.–220 C.E.), early China did not distinguish between artists and craftspeople in the modern sense. The Chinese term *gong* describes all activities ranging from jade working to iron casting and mural painting. It refers to any person making objects, whether the objects were decorated or not. The Chinese character for *gong* originally symbolized a tool.

Craftspeople, or artisans, came below scholars and farmers, but above merchants, on the social ladder. Artisans were tolerated or feared, but never truly respected. Many economic policies of the early empires were intended to strengthen agricultural production and discourage the production of crafts and commerce. Despite this, people must have realized the important role artisans played in the functioning of the state and economy. It seems that artisans made only just enough money to survive and could not be considered rich.

Artisans worked in huge outdoor workshops that were state-run operations, or in smaller indoor workshops. Private workshops produced goods for the market whereas state workshops produced goods for the ruler and aristocrats. One or two resident master artisans, who were in charge of apprentices and hired hands, ran the workshops. For many crafts, more than one artisan was necessary. Because defects could occur more easily on mass-production lines, quality-control inspections began during the Warring States Period (475–221 B.C.E.). Some areas of work were very dangerous, including metalwork, where burns and toxic gases were a constant threat. Others, such as textile and lacquer production, which were usually state-run, were less dangerous. This work was often carried out by women.

Apprentices

Apprentices were referred to as disciples and had the responsibility to transmit the master's craft to future generations. They would train for a year and take an examination at the end of year. If they passed this they would qualify for tax benefits given to the families of artisans. Artisans were either born into artisan families and continued the family occupation or family members would recommend them for training under a master.

Markets

Artisans who did not work for the state or for an aristocrat would sell their products in a market. High walls made of compacted dirt surrounded the official markets in Chang'an and other major cities. These walls had only a limited number of gates, so officials could maintain control over who was passing through them. Inside the walls were wide avenues dividing the market up into different sectors. Each sector was then divided into lanes of market stands set out according to the type of goods sold. A tower was situated in the middle of the market, decorated with a colorful flag. Officials kept an eye on the behavior of the tradesmen from the tower. The top floor housed a large drum that was struck at opening and closing times of the market.

The city of Kaifeng, bustling capital of the Song Dynasty, during the Qingming Festival.

China's First Woman Artist

Guan Daosheng (1262–1319 C.E.) was the wife of an artist and scholar-official called Zhao Mengfu. She is the first woman artist who has left behind an important collection of paintings. Guan was famous for painting bamboo, but she also painted Buddhist figures, flowers, and landscapes. She also managed all the household affairs of the family estate. She would give servants orders on which crops to plant and which dykes to repair. Guan had four children of her own, and helped raise other children in the family.

A scroll painting by Guan Daosheng titled "Bamboo Groves in Mist and Rain."

By the time of the Song Dynasty (960–1279 C.E.) the production of ceramics expanded, and workshops and kilns could be found in many areas. The most famous pieces of porcelain came from the imperial kilns in the capitals at Kaifeng and Hangzhou (*Hang-joe*), as well as Jingdezhen (*Jing-duh-jun*) in modern Jiangxi (*Jee'ang-shee*) province. Many scholar-officials were also great painters and artists during the Song.

Merchants and Traders

Merchants came at the bottom of the pecking order of the Confucian social system, which dominated most of Chinese history. This was because they were seen to produce nothing, but only to make money from the labors of others. They were often wealthy, however, and some were powerful in society.

Merchants from Chinese kingdoms and neighboring states were already trading with one another as early as the third century B.C.E. During the Han Dynasty (206 B.C.E.–220 C.E.), the Emperor Wu Di's ambassador Zhang Qian found on his travels that there was a demand for Chinese goods, especially silk, beyond the Pamir Mountains in Central Asia.

The Tang government put restrictions on merchants to stop them from becoming too powerful. They could not take civil-service examinations and therefore had no access to political power. They were rarely permitted to own land and were not allowed to ride horses.

A larger, more diverse class of merchants appeared in the Song Dynasty (960–1279 C.E.). Large commercial centers and cities also developed and multiplied in the interior and along the frontiers. Merchants' shops and craftsmen's workshops lined the streets leading out of the main cities. The administration had little control over these new enterprises. Kaifeng outgrew its original city walls. This meant a second ring of walls had to be built, and it did not take the city long to spill beyond these either. Whereas earlier major cities like Chang'an had been mainly aristocratic and administrative centers, Kaifeng was the first example of a city where commerce and amusements dominated. People started giving names to streets to make finding their way around easier, and they traveled greater distances around the country more regularly.

Transportation in the form of carts or boats became plentiful and cheap, allowing merchants to travel to different towns to buy and sell their goods. In a more mobile society, merchants

Camels were essential to merchants and travelers on the Silk Road. A camel would warn the traveler of an impending sandstorm, and could find its way to water. This terracotta figure looks foreign in appearance with large facial features and a beard.

The Silk Road

Groups of merchants traveled together along sections of Asian trade routes, which were later referred to collectively as the Silk Road (also known as the Silk Route), throughout the first millennium C.E. Very few people ever traveled the entire Silk Road. Instead, traders traveled along one section only, and sold goods to be carried to the next trading point by another merchant. Merchants rode in huge caravans of carts and camels laden with goods, and faced great dangers such as crossing war zones, being attacked by bandits, and encountering deadly desert storms. However, they could stop to buy supplies and rest their animals at desert oasis towns or at roadside inns called *caravanserai*. Communities of foreign merchants, such as the Sogdians, who came from a kingdom west of China, took up residence in Chinese cities like the Tang capital, Chang'an. All kinds of goods were traded, including silk and textiles, precious stones and jewels, foods, animals, plants, perfumes, and medicines.

This fragment of decorated silk dates from the sixth century C.E. and was discovered in a grave near Turfan, in northwest China.

began to form trading corporations called *hang*. People who took up residence away from their own hometowns would form associations of people of the same region, called *hui*. Merchants made the greatest contributions to the prosperity of the state during the Song Dynasty (960–1279 C.E.), more than at almost any time in Chinese history.

Conclusion

The far-reaching changes that had taken place by the end of the Yuan Dynasty (1279–1368 C.E.) laid the foundations for the China of modern times. Great increases in population and the scale of production led to a more complex, sophisticated society where relations between classes became more fluid. The early Ming Dynasty (1368–1644 C.E.) was a period of military and diplomatic expansion as far as Southeast Asia and the Indian Ocean. The Manchu Qing (*Ching*) Dynasty (1644–1911 C.E.) was mostly peaceful and prosperous, seeing the Chinese Empire expand to its largest since the Tang (618–907 C.E.). The decline of the Qing and the encounter with the Western world in the early twentieth century combined to overthrow the dynastic imperial system of government that had been in place for two thousand years, giving way to a turbulent period of war and revolution from which emerged the China we know today.

Glossary of Names

An Lushan military commander during the Tang Dynasty who led a rebellion which began in 755 C.E.

Chen Sheng leader of the first large-scale peasant rebellion against the Qin Dynasty

Confucius Chinese thinker and philosopher whose teachings and beliefs about compassion, loyalty, respect, sincerity, justice, and the ideal behavior of individuals, family, government, and society form the basis of Confucianism

Empress Lü wife of Liu Bang, Emperor Gaozu of the Han Dynasty; after his death in 195 B.C.E. she became very powerful

Er Shi (Huhai) son of Shi Huangdi, First Emperor of the Qin Dynasty

Gao Xianzhi Korean-born general who served under the reign of Tang Emperor Xuanzong

Genghis Khan founder of the Mongol Empire and conqueror of parts of China

Guan Daosheng important female painter, poet, and calligrapher during the Yuan Dynasty

Han Feizi member of the ruling aristocracy and philosopher who developed Xunzi's ideas into the set of beliefs and practice known as Legalism

Huang Chao leader of the Huang Chao rebellion (874–884 C.E.) that helped to bring about the eventual downfall of the Tang Dynasty

Ibn Battuta Berber scholar, traveler, and explorer from Morocco; wrote about his extensive journeys ranging from West Africa to China in the 14th century

Kangxi third emperor of the Qing Dynasty who was China's longest-reigning ruler (sixty-one years) and also considered one of its greatest emperors

King Goujian of Yue ruler of the Kingdom of Yue near the end of the Spring and Autumn Period

King Wuling of Zhao ruler of the state of Zhao during the Warring States Period

Kublai Khan fifth and last ruler of the Mongol Empire who founded the Yuan Dynasty that ruled over Mongolia, China, and some neighboring areas

Li Shimin (Taizong) second emperor of the Tang Dynasty, whose reign brought China into a period of peace and prosperity

Li Si powerful official who served under the emperors Shi Huangdi and Er Shi during the Qin Dynasty; a famous Legalist and noted calligrapher

Li Yuan (Emperor Gaozu of Tang) founder of the Tang Dynasty

Lian Po important general of the state of Zhao during the Warring States Period

Liu Bang (Emperor Gaozu of Han) former peasant who was founder and first ruler of the Han Dynasty

Marco Polo Venetian explorer and traveler famous for his journeys across Eurasia, especially those along the Silk Road to China and the Mongol Empire

Shenzong sixth emperor of the Song Dynasty

Shi Huangdi founder and first ruler of the Qin Dynasty, which unified China for the first time

Sima Qian historian, biographer, and court astrologer during the Han Dynasty

Su Shi major poet of the Song Dynasty, as well as a writer, painter, calligrapher, and official

Wang Anshi official during the reign of Song Emperor Shenzong who brought in social reforms aimed at improving the life of peasants and the unemployed

Wang Mang Han Dynasty official who briefly seized the throne and formed the Xin Dynasty, until the Han Dynasty was restored

Wu Zetian (Empress Wu of Tang) first a concubine, then wife to Emperor Gaozong; after his death, she seized the throne to become Empress from 690 C.E. to 705 C.E.

Wu Di seventh emperor of the Han Dynasty who greatly increased China's territory and organized a strong, centralized Confucian state

Xiangyu military general during the fall of the Qin Dynasty, who fought with Liu Bang for control of China

Xuanzang famous Chinese Buddhist monk, scholar, traveler, and translator during the Tang Dynasty

Xuanzong seventh and longest-reigning emperor of the Tang Dynasty

Xunzi Confucian philosopher during the Warring States Period who believed that people could improve their character through education and ritual

Yang Guifei favorite concubine of the Tang Emperor Xuanzong, killed during the An Lushan rebellion

Yang Guozhong cousin to Yang Guifei who was an official during the reign of the Emperor Xuanzong, eventually becoming chancellor before being killed during the An Lushan rebellion

Yang Jian (Wen) founder and first ruler of the Sui Dynasty who encouraged the spread of Buddhism throughout China

Zhang Qian imperial envoy and diplomat during the Han Dynasty

Zhang Yichao general who drove the occupying Tibetan forces out of the region of Dunhuang during the Tang Dynasty

Zhao (Taizu) founder and first ruler of the Song Dynasty

Zhao Kuo military general and commander of the Zhao army during the Battle of Changping between the Zhao and the Qin

Zhao Mengfu Chinese scholar, painter, and calligrapher during the Yuan Dynasty; married to Guan Daosheng

Zhenzong third emperor of the Song Dynasty and third son of Emperor Taizong (Li Shimin)

Zhu Wen military general who served under rebel leader Huang Chao, before overthrowing the Tang Dynasty in 907 C.E. and declaring himself the first emperor of the Later Liang Dynasty

Zhu Xi Confucian scholar during the Song Dynasty

Glossary

Abdicate to give up the throne

Alkali metals metals which react easily in water and to heat, used to make compounds such as saltpeter

Apprentice a trainee bound by contract to work for a specified period of time, in return for learning a master craft or skilled trade

Aristocrat member of the aristocracy; person belonging to the elite upper class of society, with status and power just below that of the emperor and empress

Artisan somebody who practices a trade or handicraft such as ceramics, jewelry-making, calligraphy, or painting

Buddhism system of religion or philosophy based on the teachings of Buddha and the path to spiritual enlightenment through ethical conduct, wisdom, and meditation

Bureaucracy administration of government through fixed rules and procedures, and organized into various departments and offices staffed with officials at varying levels of authority

Calligraphy the art of fine, stylized, or artistic writing using a pen, or a brush and ink; considered as important as painting in Chinese culture

Census complete official count or tally of the population of a country or region

Chariot open horse-drawn two-wheeled vehicle used in racing, battle, and processions

Clergy people ordained for religious service, such as priests, monks, and nuns

Concubine additional wife living with a man of higher social status, but who does not have the status and rights of an official wife

Confucianism practical system of moral, social, political, and educational philosophy based on the teachings of Confucius; Confucianism has had an important and long-lasting influence in China and other parts of East and Southeast Asia

Daoism (also spelled Taoism) system of religion or philosophy focused on the "path" or "way," which emphasizes the link between humans and nature, living a simple life, and compassion, moderation, and humility

Dignitary important person of high rank or position

Diplomacy negotiation between representatives of nations or separate groups to form alliances and agreements

Divination practice of predicting or foretelling future events, and determining the action to be taken in light of this information

Dynasty succession or series of rulers who descend from the same family

Edict formal public pronouncement or command with the force of law, made by a person in authority

Ethical relating to accepted standards of behavior and a set of beliefs and judgments of what is good and bad, and right and wrong

Feudal of or relating to a system where lords or nobles were given their own lands to control and administer, in return for allegiance and loyalty to the emperor, particularly in times of war

Filial piety person's love, respect, and duty toward his or her parents, grandparents, and ancestors; a virtue to be practiced by everyone, and still considered important in Chinese society today

Garrison military post, usually permanent, originally designed to guard a specific place such as a town, city, or castle; also, the troops assigned to that post

Granary building used as a storehouse for grain

Hemp tall cultivated plant with tough fibers that are used to make rope, paper, canvas, and other textiles

Inflation continual rise in the general price for goods and services over time, so that more money is needed to buy the same amount

Legalism system of philosophy and government that held the law as the supreme authority and that everyone was equal under the law. Laws were written down and made public, and had to be strictly and rigidly followed; anyone breaking the law was severely punished, even in the face of natural justice, mercy, or commonsense

Mandate the command, authority, or right to act in a certain role

Maritime on, near, or relating to the sea; seagoing; of or relating to shipping and navigating by sea

Missionary person sent by a religious organization to convert others to their faith

Pastoral of or relating to rural people who live as shepherds and herders, raising and breeding domesticated animals such as sheep and cattle

Plastron almost-flat breastbone, or underside, of a tortoise or turtle shell that protects the soft abdomen

Polo game played by two teams of players on horseback, where the object is to drive a hard white ball through the opposition's goal using long-handled mallets

Porcelain hard, mostly white translucent ceramic made by firing clay and other materials in a kiln at high temperatures

Prefecture district or province

Reincarnated reborn after death as another living being; reincarnation, or rebirth, is a concept found in the practice of Buddhism and other religions

Saltpeter potassium nitrate, a chemical used in gunpowder and explosives, fireworks, fertilizers, and to preserve or cure meat

Scholar learned and well-educated person, often with advanced knowledge in a special area or field of study

Sogdian relating to a kingdom, called Sogdia, made up of several city states in Central Asia, including Samarkand

Standing army permanent fighting force maintained in times of both peace and war

Steppe huge flat and mostly treeless area covered in grasslands, found in parts of Central Asia, southeastern Europe, and Siberia

Transcribe make a full written copy; represent speech in written form as words or characters

Learn More About

Books

Art, Suzanne Strauss. *The Story of Ancient China.* Lincoln, Mass: Pemblewick Press, 2001

Art, Suzanne Strauss. *China's Later Dynasties.* Lincoln, Mass: Pemblewick Press, 2002

Challen, Paul. *Life in Ancient China (Peoples of the Ancient World).* New York: Crabtree PC, 2004

Cotterell, Arthur & Buller, Laura. *Ancient China (DK Eyewitness Books).* New York: Dorling Kindersley, 2005

Ebrey, Patricia B. *The Cambridge Illustrated History of China (Cambridge Illustrated Histories).* New York: Cambridge University Press, 1999

Einfeld, Jann. *Exploring Cultural History—Living in Imperial China (Exploring Cultural History).* San Diego, CA: Greenhaven Press, 2004

Freedman, Russell. *Confucius: The Golden Rule.* New York: Arthur A Levine Books, 2002

Hall, Eleanor J. *Ancient Chinese Dynasties (World History).* San Diego, CA: Greenhaven, 2000

Portal, Jane. *The First Emperor: China's Terracotta Army.* Cambridge, Mass: Harvard University Press, 2007

Turnbull, Stephen. *The Great Wall of China 221BC –1644AD (Fortress).* New York: Osprey Publishing 2007

Schomp, Virginia. *The Ancient Chinese (People of the Ancient World).* New York: Franklin Watts, 2005

Shu, Shin Lu & Zhou, Kate. *The People of China: The History and Culture of China.* Broomall, PA: Mason Crest Publishers, 2005

Web Sites

Asterius—Chinese History
http://asterius.com/china/

British Museum—Ancient China
www.ancientchina.co.uk

British Museum—Early Imperial China
www.earlyimperialchina.co.uk

Brooklyn College—Chinese History
http://acc6.its.brooklyn.cuny.edu/~phalsall/texts/chinhist.html

China Knowledge—Chinese History
www.chinaknowledge.de/History/history.htm

Saint Martin's University—China through History in Maps
http://homepages.stmartin.edu/Fac_Staff/rlangill/HIS%20217/HIS%20217%20Maps.htm

San Jose State University—Legalism
www.applet-magic.com/legalism.htm

Shanghai American School—Ancient China
http://sasasianhistory.wetpaint.com/page/Life+in+Ancient+China?t=anon

University of Maryland—Chinese History
www-chaos.umd.edu/history/toc.html

Washington State University—Imperial China
www.wsu.edu:8080/~dee/CHEMPIRE/CONTENTS.HTM

Index